The Norwich Shawl

Its History
and a Catalogue of the Collection
at Strangers Hall Museum, Norwich

PAMELA CLABBURN

with contributions from
PENELOPE ALFREY, RACHEL CHAPLE, HELEN HOYTE,
URSULA PRIESTLEY AND JUDY WENTWORTH

Norfolk Museums Service

LONDON: HMSO

Applications for reproduction should be made to HMSO
Copyright Unit, St Crispins, Duke Street,
Norwich NR3 1PD

ISBN 0 11 701584 9 (paperback)
ISBN 0 11 701591 1 (cased edition)

British Library Cataloguing in Publication Data
A CIP catalogue record for this book is available from
the British Library.

Design: HMSO Graphic Design

Norfolk Museums Service is a joint service provided by
the County and District Councils

Cover illustration (*top to bottom*): catalogue nos 104, 32
and 82.

Published by HMSO and available from:

HMSO Publications Centre
(Mail, fax and telephone orders only)
PO Box 276, London SW8 5DT
Telephone orders 0171 873 9090
General enquiries 0171 873 0011
(queuing system in operation for both numbers)
Fax orders 0171 873 8200

HMSO Bookshops
49 High Holborn, London WC1V 6HB
(counter service only)
0171 873 0011   Fax 0171 831 1326
68–69 Bull Street, Birmingham B4 6AD
0121 236 9696   Fax 0121 236 9699
33 Wine Street, Bristol BS1 2BQ
0117 926 4306   Fax 0117 929 4515
9–21 Princess Street, Manchester M60 8AS
0161 834 7201   Fax 0161 833 0634
16 Arthur Street, Belfast BT1 4GD
01232 238451   Fax 01232 235401
71 Lothian Road, Edinburgh EH3 9AZ
0131 228 4181   Fax 0131 229 2734
The HMSO Oriel Bookshop
The Friary, Cardiff CF1 4AA
01222 395548   Fax 01222 384347

HMSO's Accredited Agents
(see Yellow Pages)

and through good booksellers

Printed in the United Kingdom for HMSO
Dd 299911 C15 8/95

Contents

Notes on Contributors

Pamela Clabburn was Curator of Strangers Hall Museum, Norwich, from 1964 to 1974. Upon retirement, she started the Textile Conservation Workroom at Blickling Hall, Norfolk, for the National Trust's Eastern Region, and worked there until 1984. During this period and after her second retirement, Pamela has written prolifically on textiles and is the author of: *The Needleworker's Dictionary, Samplers, Beadwork, Masterpieces of Embroidery, Shawls, Patchwork, The National Trust Book of Furnishing Textiles* and various articles on costume and textiles.

Penelope Alfrey studied art history at the University of Edinburgh and trained in textile conservation at the Victoria & Albert Museum under Sheila Landi. She has wide experience as a freelance textile conservator and consultant on textile and dress collections in the East Midlands region. She is a full-time lecturer at Loughborough College of Art & Design, with a special interest in dress and appearance, and is currently researching into the shawl as a symbol of femininity in 18th- and 19th-century French and English culture.

Rachel Chaple's interest in textiles derived from both sides of her family, but particularly her mother's descent from Belfast linen manufacturers. She obtained a degree in sociology from Goldsmith's College, London, in 1976 and then took up weaving, with particular interest in old looms, machinery and the history of weaving. She subsequently took the Bradford certificate in handloom weaving, spinning and dyeing in 1980 and City and Guilds qualifications in creative studies in textiles in 1980 and 1981, before moving to Norfolk where she taught weaving in Adult Education. She now lives in Norwich.

Helen M Hoyte has worked as a textile designer, taught crafts in a school of occupational therapy and taught art to A-level in a large comprehensive school. She has lectured to groups in Further Education on the history of art and on costume and textiles. She has also held exhibitions of her own embroidery and painting and has designed costumes for local grand opera. Now retired, Helen is Chairman of the Costume and Textile Association for Norfolk Museums.

Ursula Priestley holds an MA in Natural Sciences from the University of Cambridge and a further one in Local and Regional History from the University of East Anglia (UEA). From 1976 to 1982 she was a researcher for the Norfolk Survey, an archaeological and documentary project conducted by the city and the Centre of East Anglian Studies (CEAS) at UEA. Since 1984 Ursula has been researching into the Norwich textile industry under the auspices of the CEAS, where she is an Honorary Research Fellow. Her publications include: *The Great Market: A Survey of Nine Hundred Years of Norwich Provision Market, The Fabric of Stuffs: The Norwich Textile Industry from 1565* and *The Letters of Philip Stannard, Norwich Textile Manufacturer (1751–1763)*; and she has also contributed to the journals *Post-Medieval Archaeology, Textile History, Costume, The London Journal* and *Fabrics and Fashions*.

Judy Wentworth has been a full-time antique dealer for most of her adult life. For the past fifteen years she has specialised in textiles, co-operating with many museums in the UK and abroad. From 1981 to 1993 she and her partner Sarah Franklyn ran a specialist shop, The Antique Textile Company, in Holland Park, London. They mounted exhibitions on shawls, lace, silks, printed cottons and bedcovers. Judy is the author of *Quilts*, gives occasional lectures and contributes articles and reviews to trade publications. She lives and works in London, where she now owns The Textile Company.

Acknowledgements

The author and Norfolk Museums Service wish to thank the Worshipful Company of Dyers for their contribution towards the cost of this publication.

A large catalogue such as this cannot be made without the help of a large number of people. Firstly, hearty thanks are due to members of the Costume and Textile Association for Norfolk Museums. They have worked with a will and great dedication, especially the Chairman Helen Hoyte and members of the Committee. Audrey Kinder, Jan Miller, Phyll Oates, Faye Groom and Pat Shearman trawled through back numbers of the newspapers, mostly before the disastrous fire at Norwich Central Library in August 1994, and retrieved much information. The staff at Strangers Hall Museum, where the shawls are stored, have been kind and long-suffering towards too many people invading the very small space in which to work. And in another direction, Molly Barrett of Em En Designs who turned my impossible writing into readable printouts, and Ruth Bowden who combined charm and editorial firmness at HMSO, deserve my best thanks.

Foreword

It is with much pleasure that I write the foreword to this publication. The shawls have been selected from the important collection of costume and textiles in the Strangers Hall Museum, Norwich. Sadly, due to the restrictions of space, the public can only see a small fraction of the wealth and variety of the collection now stored in this charming museum of social history.

The shawls were manufactured in Norwich, and though famous in the 19th century for the excellence of their design and the technical expertise applied in their manufacture, they have remained largely unrecognised except by textile specialists. For too long the once-significant textile industry, which was the life blood of Norwich for many years, has been neglected.

This book and the exhibition it accompanies show clearly that Norwich shawls deserve the same recognition as that enjoyed by those made in Paisley and France. One can only be impressed by the style and splendour of these beautiful shawls.

Not only does this book make a significant contribution to the history of Norwich, but also to British social and fashion history and to the history of European textile manufacture. It is also an enduring testimony to the dedication and professionalism of Pamela Clabburn and also to her many colleagues, namely the contributors to this volume, Fiona Strodder and the staff at Strangers Hall Museum and the members of the Costume and Textile Association for Norfolk Museums. The combined efforts of all these people will ensure that the Norwich shawl and textile industry are firmly placed on the map of history.

It is my hope that both the information given here and the exhibition will provide a marvellous opportunity to bring the quality and historical value of this important collection to a wider audience, and in time, that it may be on permanant exhibition and more easily accessible to students.

Catherine Wilson
Director
Norfolk Museums Service

Notes for the Reader

A NOTE ON TERMS

The book contains terms used in different textile-manufacturing centres for the motifs most commonly associated with shawl designs. The regional variations are given below.

Norwich	pine
Paisley	Paisley pine or the Paisley
India	*buta* or *boteh*
France	palmette

Terms denoting a shawl with four quarter-circles in the corners, with or without a centre circle:

Norwich	pot lid
Paisley	medallion
India	moon
France	rosace

Terms denoting a semicircular shawl with a tassel hanging from the centre of the straight side:

Costume definition	*burnous*
Norwich	Arab shawl
Paisley	Glasgow shawl

The following terms are exclusive to the Norwich shawl industry:

Fillover	The pattern woven or darned into the plain ground of a shawl, usually with wool.
Chinese Architectural	A design in clear straightforward colours, having a distinct Chinese look. Generally found in shawl borders of the 1830s.
Exotic flower	A design with sprays of imaginative flowers and foliage.
Naturalistic flower	A design with flowers and foliage which are recognisable as species.

THE CATALOGUE

The shawls fall into six natural groupings, reflected in the Catalogue: turnover shawls and Chinese Architectural designs; shawls by Towler & Campin; Arab shawls; shawls by Clabburn, Sons & Crisp; shawls woven by James Churchyard; and miscellaneous shawls.

Catalogue entries are, broadly speaking, ordered chronologically within each of the six sections.

The second line of each catalogue-entry heading gives the date of maufacture of each shawl. The third line records the depth and width of each shawl – the longest measurement is always given first.

Records kept by Strangers Hall Museum, Norwich, where possible, record the names of the donors and vendors of shawls. Some wish their name to be shown (so they can point it out to their children and friends), others prefer to be anonymous. The wishes of the donor or vendor are always considered when names are published.

SOURCES

The Norfolk Local History Library archives, and many other books, newspapers and documents, were sadly destroyed in a fire which gutted Norwich Central Library in August 1994. Fortunately, much of the research and writing for this volume had by then been carried out. However, it has not been possible to give full references for some of the bibliographical and archival material cited in the book.

Introduction

The exhibition has drawn on the large collection housed in the Strangers Hall Museum which includes shawls, not only those made in Norwich but shawls from Paisley, France and India. Strangers Hall, the earliest part of which is the undercroft dating from the early 14th century, has, over the centuries, been added to, adapted and changed to suit its many owners. In its present role as a museum, it reflects changes in architecture and furnishings which visitors can appreciate in the various rooms dedicated to individual periods.

This publication, which is a vital part of the exhibition, attempts to put together all that is known of the shawl industry in the city, its weavers, manufacturers, trade and social history. It has not been an easy task for various reasons, but mainly because of the almost complete dearth of information on the 19th-century Norwich manufacturers. From an exhaustive examination of trade directories, census returns, rate books and newspapers very little, apart from names and addresses, could be found, though from these sources the names of well over a hundred manufacturers were gathered (see Appendix). There was rivalry and jealousy between firms, and in most cases records were burnt. This problem was not resolved until the Companies Act was passed in 1923, requiring manufacturers to keep records for public viewing. In a few cases the records had been kept, some of which were later donated to the city by public-spirited owners and are today stored in the Bridewell Museum in Norwich. These provide a basis of historical fact.

Norwich in medieval times was the second city in the kingdom, and for many centuries depended for its livelihood on the flourishing textile industry centred in the city and in the surrounding villages. Several waves of immigrants in the 16th and 17th centuries brought their expertise from other weaving countries, particularly Flanders (the Dutch and Walloons) and northern France. Weavers from these countries, known locally as Strangers, brought their considerable weaving skills with them, eventually settled and were assimilated by the local community. Their particular expertise was in weaving what were known as half-silks, i.e., light dress-weight fabrics made from a mixture of yarns, either wool and silk, wool and cotton or sometimes wool and linen. The fabrics made from these yarns were generally strongly patterned, either with stripes in bright colours or with floral designs, and were often hot-pressed, which gave them a strikingly glossy surface and added much to their attraction. In the late 18th and all through the 19th century the trade in shawls, mostly woven from two yarns and intricately patterned, fitted perfectly into the framework for weaving manufacture already established in the city.

The term 'Norwich shawl' has always been used by the city itself, to denote a shawl made in imitation of the Indian style. These were of many designs according to the fashion of the day. Generally the designs included a representation of the Indian pine or *buta*, but these motifs were not exclusive to the shawls made in Norwich. Edinburgh, Paisley and France, as well as other Continental countries, made use of the motif in their designs. In 1847 the order books of E & F Hinde show the names of twenty-nine styles of shawl. We do not know what the styles were, but it is likely most of them would not have been classed as typical of the 'Norwich shawl' style.

In 1855 the retailer G L Coleman, advertising shawls made by Towler & Campin, cites the 'Levantine, Grenadine, Long Printed, Cantons, Stellas, Printed Baregas, Llama, Norwich Fillings and Printed Cashmeres'. All of these shawls were made in Norwich by one firm, but only the Long, Norwich Fillings and Printed Cashmeres could be termed Norwich shawls.

Shawls are notoriously difficult to date accurately, which is why they are so often catalogued as 'the 1840s' or '1820–30' or even, in desperation, '1820–1840'. Style is a pointer to date, but there are many shawls which did not follow fashion quickly or were designed and made either by an old-fashioned manufacturer or, alternatively, by one who was distinctly avant-garde.

Before 1842 the only help in dating comes from the all-too-few portraits, fashion plates or engravings where shawls can be seen clearly, from the very few pattern books extant or from family history. The first two can be helpful, but it is unwise to rely too heavily on the last as memories of the generations can be faulty. Hence the vagueness of dating. It is easier to date shawls manufactured after 1842, as in this year it became possible to register designs in the Public Record Office (PRO). Thus, 315 Norwich designs of both woven and printed shawls were registered, and the designs can still be examined at the PRO. However, a large number of manufacturers, for reasons not known, did not consider registration worthwhile. But those who did register have provided the Museum with fixed points of reference and from these we can place further shawls which, though we are reasonably sure are in fact Norwich-made, we label as 'probably' or even 'possibly' Norwich.

This book comprises two main parts. The essays in Part One describe the historical background and show from various angles how this large and important part of the textile trade of the city of Norwich grew. Part Two presents the shawl collection and is followed by an Appendix giving as much detail as possible on the manufacturers and their changes of name and work places. The exhibition provides a unique opportunity to put the shawls on display together, and it is hoped that, as a consequence, more people will realise that they are the owners of a valuable Norwich shawl. If an impeccable provenance can be established for a shawl, this adds considerably to our knowledge of what was and was not made in Norwich.

PART ONE

Background to

the Norwich Shawl

1 *The Norwich Textile Industry*
1750–1880

URSULA PRIESTLEY

The creation in the 19th century of the famous Norwich shawls, with their vivid colours and intricate designs, marked the peak of artistic and technical achievement of an industry which had evolved its skills in the production of patterned fabrics over three centuries. The origins of textile manufacture in Norwich are, of course, found much earlier than the 16th century, but it was only after the arrival in the city in 1565 of a group of immigrant weavers from the Low Countries that figured designs in mixed colours became a feature of the industry's repertoire. The 'Strangers', as they were always known, were invited – with the sanction of Queen Elizabeth – to settle in Norwich with a view to revitalising textile manufacture, which had been at a low ebb after several years of serious economic difficulty. These Dutch and Walloon (French-speaking) craftsmen brought with them the so-called New Draperies, a mixed range of fabrics already popular on the Continent, but some of which were new to Norwich. The initial group of hard-working Strangers were soon joined by others, and by the turn of the century there was indeed a revival in the city's textile trade.

From some of the New Draperies (especially those made by the Walloons) were developed the distinctive worsted textiles which became known in the 17th century as Norwich Stuffs. Characteristically, they were beautifully designed, colourful, and very varied fabrics, many of them with patterns of flowers, checks, and shaded stripes. Some of the more elaborate figures needed to be woven on the drawloom, the introduction of which can also probably be credited to the Strangers. The drawloom was an adaptation of the handloom, by which the warp threads could be raised in a pre-arranged sequence with the help of a worker known as a drawboy. It continued in use for the manufacture of patterned fabrics – virtually unchanged – until the invention of the Jacquard loom in the 19th century.

Although Norwich Stuffs were basically worsted, many of them incorporated other yarns such as linen, mohair or silk, giving scope for wide variation of the appearance and feel of the end product. They were aimed at a fashionable, middle-income clientele such as minor country gentry, provincial merchants and wealthy yeomen, and were bought for gowns, bodices, petticoats, men's suits and waistcoats, and also for furnishings. The great strengh of the industry lay in the ability of the master weavers to diversify their fabrics in line with the changing tastes of their customers.

Thus evolved a highly skilled and specialist trade, in many respects unique to the city of Norwich. Increasingly, the widespread use of silk yarns, giving a sparkle or lustre to the product, became the hallmark of the industry, and by the end of the 17th century Norwich was acknowledged as the chief centre for the manufacture of silk-and-worsted mixtures, or 'half-silks' as they were also called. By this time textile production overwhelmingly dominated the city's economy, and would continue to do so throughout the 18th century.

By 1750 Norwich Stuffs had developed a high degree of refinement and sophistication. They were made in an extraordinary diversity of texture, weave and pattern, using worsted yarns of the most superior quality, dyed in the range of bright colours for which the city was famous. Designs for the luxury end of the trade were carefully chosen with fashion in mind, and were probably purchased from draftsmen in London; some followed styles similar to those found in contemporary French silks. The earliest surviving pattern books and samples date from this period, enabling at least some of the 18th-century stuffs to be analysed and classified. The most elaborate and expensive were brocaded satins, in which extra, or 'floating' warp threads produced designs of large, stylised flowers and fruit on a satin-weave background. Similar were tapizadoes, distinguished by their exceptionally brilliant colours. Worsted damasks, recorded as having been made in Norwich as early as the 1580s, were self-coloured fabrics, the pattern made by contrasting weft and warp faces of the weave. Taboretts (sometimes known as brilliants) and florettas had smaller sprigged figures on plain or patterned backgrounds, while chiveretts and diamantines were woven in chevron and diamond designs, often in two or more colours. Perhaps the best known of all the Norwich specialities were callimancoes, whose vivid, rainbow-shaded stripes were woven in many colours.

Most of the figured stuffs made in the 18th century were given body and a high gloss by hot-pressing. This was a complicated and skilled procedure. It involved folding the finished pieces concertina fashion, and interleaving them with sheets of cardboard, specially treated, usually with gum arabic. Between the cardboard were placed iron plates that had been heated in a furnace, and the pile was strongly compressed using a heavy screw press. The resulting smooth glaze, besides being fashionable, had the dubious secondary benefit of concealing faults and flaws in the yarn or weave.

Not all Norwich products were elaborately patterned. Camblets were of ancient origin and had been a staple of the trade for many years. They were close-textured, plain-weave fabrics finished in a variety of ways and sometimes incorporating simple checks or stripes; some patterned versions were known as cambletees, and there were many

A Norwich-made multicoloured worsted damask of c.1790. In the petals the lines of twill weave are very evident, as they were later in the woven shawls. When shawls were printed, the lines were put into the design as hatching in order to make them look like their expensive woven counterparts.
BRIDEWELL MUSEUM, NORWICH

other names for recognised variations.

In parallel with the manufacture of coloured stuffs, Norwich was much involved in the production of mourning fabrics, or the 'Black Branch' as it was known. The industry's contributions to the trade were bombazine and Norwich crêpe, both, in their black form, in growing demand throughout the 18th century and well into the 19th. Bombazine was a silk-and-worsted mixture, made in a twill weave with the worsted warp uppermost, giving the matt, densely black appearance considered obligatory for the rituals of deep mourning. Norwich crêpe, consistently a best-seller among the city's wares, was also made of silk and worsted, but was lighter in weight, and woven from yarns twisted to give a puckered effect. Bombazine was used for dress, Norwich crêpe mostly for veils, scarves and hatbands; although the latter, when made with heavy crimping, was known as 'burying crêpe', and could be used for gowns for the funeral. Demand for mourning fabrics was relatively stable – an important counterbalance to the unreliability of the fashion trade in coloured stuffs.

All told, the structure of the Norwich textile industry in the 18th century was notably complex, its firms making many different types of product, often calling not only for advanced technical skills, but also for ingenuity and constant innovation in order to keep abreast of fickle customer demand. Because of the specialist nature of the trade, Norwich was historically a city of small and medium-sized businesses, each an independent, self-financing, family-based unit operating with only a few looms. Typically, the owner was a fully trained master weaver, who would expect to exercise day-to-day surveillance of all aspects of manufacture, and who would find a buyer for his goods himself. The industry was essentially urban-based and closely integrated, its organisation in many ways unique to Norwich. Businesses often remained in the same family for several generations and skills were passed down from father to son, and uncle to nephew.

This old industrial pattern was beginning to

French-designed dresses of the 1880s showing the use of crêpe in the three stages of mourning. In the first year (left) the costume is about 75 per cent crêpe, in the second year (centre) the amount used is considerably lessened, and by the third year (right) there are only touches of crêpe, in this case in the hat. By the end of the third year, however, there might well be another death, either of a child, an in-law, or a remoter relation, when the amount of crêpe would again have to be increased, and it could be several years more before the widow was able to exchange black for a different colour of attire. Hence the excellent sales of crêpe.

change by the 1750s. Since the 1720s, expanding trade, especially in the field of exports, had brought growing profits for the most successful of the Norwich manufacturers; assets had built up, while judicious mergers and partnerships meant that firms tended to be larger and fewer, consolidating the fragmented structure of earlier years. Nevertheless, daily supervision of the complicated processes of production by an experienced master remained of paramount importance. The manufacturer's own residence was the hub of operations. Usually he lived in a handsome house abutting on the street, with a counting-house, packing-rooms, warehouses, and often a hot-pressing shop to the rear. Only weaving and dyeing took place off the premises. The 18th-century manufacturer made extensive use of the 'putting-out' system. In other words, he employed an army of skilled journeymen weavers, at times as many as 300–400, recruited as required and paid on piece-rates. They worked under his direct control, but used their own looms in their own houses. This accords with the picture of the city in the mid-18th century attributed to William Taylor, a German scholar and writer, who, as a young man, worked briefly in the family textile business. He wrote this passage in 1798 referring to an earlier age: 'Norwich was now crowded with looms. Every winter's evening exhibited to the traveller entering its walls the appearance of a general illumination' (R Beatniffe, *The Norfolk Tour*, Norwich, 1808, p 94). There is further confirmation in the first-hand account by the Marchioness Grey of her visit to East Anglia in 1750:

> I was disappointed in not being able to see any of their Manufactures at Norwich. I expected to have seen some kind of Public buildings for carrying them on, or large Workrooms belonging to the several weavers, but there is no such thing, and the Workmen I was told all have their separate Looms in their own houses; and mounting up into a garret to see a single Loom was not worth while. ('Journal of the Marchioness Grey', Bedfordshire Record Office, Ref.L30/21/3/8)

Today, the organising abilities of Norwich masters needed to harness and direct such a large and dispersed workforce seem remarkable – one of the unsung talents of the 18th century.

Bright, attractive colours were essential to the saleability of Norwich Stuffs. The presence in Norwich of a handful of expert dyers, nationally known for the excellence and permanence of their dyes, was one of the industry's great strengths. They undertook work from all over the country as well as from the city's manufacturers.

Continuing expansion of the export trade meant that, for most of the city's manufacturers, the mid-18th century was a time of growth and mounting success. As Arthur Young put it in 1771: 'From 1743 to 1763 was their famous era' (*A Farmer's Tour through the East of England*, London, 1771, vol.2, p 74). This idea of an industrial golden age lingered on, and was echoed by other commentators in the 19th century. In time, Norwich products reached most of the developed world. At first, much of the accelerating trade was with Europe. Some of the cheaper stuffs were hugely popular in central and northern Germany and the Baltic countries in what might be termed a peasant market. Their lively colours and wide variety of sprigged and flowery patterns gave them great appeal for regional and village dress (or what we would now call folk costume), each community choosing its own distinctive design for bodices, waistcoats and dresses. In the 1760s the stuff trade was extended into Poland and Russia. In particular, negotiations with Russia revealed enormous commercial potential, since the rainbow-shaded callimancoes were much sought after by Tartar and Siberian tribes for sashes.

In Italy, a well-established demand for the lighter-weight stuffs continued, and there was a strong and growing market for camblets and stuffs in the Iberian peninsula. From Spain, Norwich goods, in increasing volume, were re-exported to the West Indies, Mexico and the Americas. Outside Europe, regular annual orders from the East India Company for camblets for India and the Far East provided the industry with a valuable bulwark against the fluctuation of markets elsewhere.

Until the mid-18th century, the bulk of this widespread overseas trade passed through the hands of the London dealers. It was a system that had many advantages for Norwich manufacturers, pre-occupied as they were with the technicalities of production in their workshops in the city. They had easy access by post to the large pool of merchants in the capital, many of them exporters trading on an international scale and resident representatives of foreign firms dealing in textiles. Goods destined for export were usually made to the order of the agent concerned, who was able to choose designs from regularly updated pattern swatches supplied from Norwich. Bales of stuff were loaded on to waggons and travelled by frequent scheduled carrier services along the good turnpike road to London which terminated in Bishopsgate, arriving three to four days later. After the delivery of the goods in the capital, the responsibility of the manufacturers ended. They paid a good rate of commission to the agents concerned, and in return were able to avoid the innumerable pitfalls inherent in shipping overseas – irregular sailing times, unpredictable and often adverse weather conditions, customs and tariffs, insurance, foreign political upheavals and wars, and above all the essential need to have recourse to sufficient circulating capital to sustain long-term credit.

None the less, by about 1760 trading mechanisms were beginning to change. For various reasons, including, it was said, the large extent of speculative trading by Norwich firms, the London channel had become less attractive. Goods were stockpiled in the capital's warehouses, creating a bottleneck which had repercussions back in Norwich. Moreover, the bigger master weavers coveted the gains pocketed by the London dealers; and by that time a number had accumulated sufficient reserves through years of trading via London to be able to accept a greater degree of financial risk. Some of the more enterprising, inexperienced though they were in overseas marketing, began tentatively to correspond directly with foreign firms.

As they became independent of the London middlemen, many Norwich firms greatly extended their already lucrative business on the Continent. To quote William Taylor again: 'Their travellers penetrated through Europe, and their pattern-books were exhibited in every principal town, from the frozen plains of Moscow, to the milder climes of Lisbon, Seville, and Naples . . . The great fairs of Frankfort, Leipsic and of Salerno [*sic*], were thronged with the purchasers of these [Norwich] commodities' (Beatniffe, *The Norfolk Tour*, p 94).

The masters in Norwich were visited by

overseas buyers, and some travelled abroad themselves, acquiring a wide circle of foreign acquaintances. Often, they had been sent abroad as young men (as indeed had William Taylor) to learn a language and foster their fathers' business connections – travels which could be combined with the Grand Tour. They returned with a wider understanding of the countries they had visited and with knowledge and appreciation of Continental art and culture. As they continued to augment their fortunes, the city's manufacturers, as a class, gained a reputation in the textile world for being not only wealthy and influential, but also the most intelligent and cultivated industrialists in the country.

During these prosperous middle years of the 18th century, an air of affluence pervaded Norwich. Many of the echoes of Georgian grandeur to be seen in the present-day city date from this period. Elegant houses built, or embellished, by manufacturers are to be found in St George Colegate and St Giles parishes, and in Surrey Street, and opulently carved memorials, naming them as merchants (as they were by then entitled to call themselves) hang on the walls of their parish churches. They were noted for their beneficence, and such cherished city buildings as the Assembly House and the Octagon Chapel were founded on textile-generated riches.

Foreign wars in the 1760s and 1770s brought setbacks and an end to this era of growth and prosperity. A skirmish with Spain in 1762, in the last stages of the Seven Years War, interfered with shipping to the Iberian Peninsula, and some of those manufacturers who had developed a regular trade with Spanish merchants found their goods held up in the London warehouses. This meant that production in Norwich had to be cut back, resulting in lay-offs and unemployment.

Potentially much more serious, because of the vulnerability of the rapidly developing trade with the Americas, was the American War of Independence, 1775–83. Although begun as an internal dispute between England and her New World colonies, the War drew in other nations, notably France and Spain. Exports were disrupted by the presence of foreign navies in the Channel and by harassment by American privateers of merchant ships bound for Spain. In the short term, considerable damage was caused to overseas trade.

But there was also trouble at home. Although overshadowed by export success, the domestic market for worsted stuffs had never lost its place as the industry's vital second string, and towards the end of the century found its position in the dress-fabric trade dangerously undermined by a rapid expansion of the cotton industry. With the advance of Lancashire manufacture in the wake of mechanisation, cotton goods became cheaper and more readily available. Their advantages compared with worsted products, however fine, were manifest. The price differential was the most obvious. But there were others. Customers were wary of the highly glazed Norwich Stuffs, since not only could they not be washed, they had a tendency to spot in the rain. Muslins and cambrics provided a practical alternative for general wear, and soon became universally popular. At the same time, printed cotton fabrics supplanted worsteds and worsted mixtures for hangings and curtains. In 1784 Norwich attempted to retaliate by establishing local cotton weaving, making shirtings, muslins and cambrics of excellent quality and dye, but although the venture was successful for a time, it seems never to have reached its full potential, and petered out in the early years of the 19th century.

An even more insidious long-term threat to the heartland of Norwich worsted manufacture came in the form of competition from the West Riding of Yorkshire. The northern worsted trade had been developing steadily since the early 1700s, especially in the manufacture of the simpler and coarser worsted stuffs, and by 1750, at a time when Norwich weavers were still tied to an export trade using the London dealers, enterprising Yorkshire merchants were shipping vast amounts of textiles overseas from the port of Hull. Thus, for the North, the mechanisms for rapid recovery after the end of the American War were already in place. In the 1750s anxieties were being voiced in the Norwich newspapers about the encroaching danger

of northern competition, but Yorkshire goods were dismissed as being of inferior quality. Towards the end of the century, however, rivalry became more acute, as ambitious weavers in the West Riding, notably in Halifax, began to introduce the finer kinds of Norwich manufactures into their repertoire, directly copying some of the more successful lines such as bombazines, camblets and damasks.

The industry was never to return fully to the profitability of the golden years of the mid-18th century. Nevertheless, it was said that, for twelve or more years following the end of the American War in 1783, 'some of the lustre of its meridian' was regained (letter by 'Senex', *East Anglian Newspaper*, 21 February 1832). Patterned stuffs were again made in great quantity and variety for the European and American markets; new luxury fabrics were created for the domestic trade; some manufacturers continued to execute huge orders for camblets for the East India Company; demand for Norwich crêpes and bombazines remained buoyant; and shawl manufacture was introduced for the first time. Legend has it that cock-a-hoop weavers flaunted their riches by sporting five-pound notes tucked into their hat-bands.

This prosperous interlude was short-lived. From 1793 to 1815 the great Continental wars that followed the French Revolution seriously eroded the city's European trade. A newspaper report on the state of textile manufacture in 1816, the year following peace, was depressing: 'Since the commencement of the War, the manufactory of Norwich has undergone a revolution almost as complete as any of the foreign states for whom her citizens were at that period engaged' (*Norwich Mercury*, 28 April 1817). In the view of the writer, the vast foreign trade that had been built up before the War, carried on by manufacturers in extensive businesses, had been, by degrees, suspended and finally lost, with the exception of that area of the trade which served the East India Company. Cotton and worsted weaving were 'almost at a total stand' (*ibid.*). Nevertheless, the survey was not wholly pessimistic. Norwich mercantile talent was reasserting itself, and new businesses were springing up, making a variety of products. Prominent among these were shawl manufacture and 'a most magnificent establishment for crapes and gauzes' (*ibid.*).

The account is a pointer to the direction the industry would take in the 19th century. Shawl manufacture, and the production of mourning fabrics, especially a new form of Norwich crêpe made from pure silk gauze, sustained the city's textile economy until the 1880s. Without them, the industry's decline would have been even more rapid.

Demand for the elaborately patterned and heavily glazed stuffs that had been so popular for peasant dress in northern Europe and Scandinavia never revived after the Napoleonic Wars. They were considered obsolete and were no longer made in Norwich. It was a serious loss of a once immensely lucrative overseas market. But the manufacture of worsted and worsted-mixture dress fabrics was by no means at a permanent standstill. The years after the Treaty of Paris in 1815 saw the creation of some of the finest and most beautiful of all Norwich textiles – mainly aimed at the home market. The first of these was invented in 1819 by a Mr Francis, and christened Norwich crêpe; it was a finely woven silk and worsted mixture, made 'in the grey', dyed in the widest possible range of colours, and finished to imitate rich satin. (It must not be confused with the pure silk mourning crêpe already mentioned, which was not introduced until 1822.) The new coloured crêpe was aimed at a high-class clientele, and indeed, was promoted at a Crape Ball held at the Assembly House in 1826, and attended by many notable Norfolk worthies. Other fine-textured innovations followed, such as crêpe de Lyon, poplin français, challis, and many more. Sadly, most were ephemeral, remaining in fashion for only one or two seasons.

The 1820s and 1830s were very difficult years for the Norwich industry. Erratic sales of the new products brought cycles of activity followed by slump, which meant periodic deprivation for the workers, many of whom had to resort to poor relief. The situation was exacerbated by the loss of the close commercial link with the East India Company. When the Company's Charter was renewed by the Government in 1813, the monopoly of trade with India was lost, and the market thrown open. Orders for Norwich camblets became steadily smaller and fewer and, when a further renewal in 1833 removed restrictions on trade with China, they ceased altogether. Future exporters cared less about quality than price, buying camblets where they were cheapest – in Yorkshire.

The losses were compensated for, in some degree, by the increasing production of shawls and mourning fabrics.

The evolution of the shawl industry, described elsewhere, was propelled by a number of technical advances, and Norwich shawls became renowned world-wide for their superb quality, design and workmanship. They sold for high prices, making large profits for their creators, and earning good wages for weavers with the required level of skill.

Of equal significance as the 19th century progressed was the old staple trade in bombazine and crêpe. Bombazine had continued in production throughout the war with Napoleon and, despite slumps in the 1820s due to over-stocking and gloomy predictions that this profitable product would be superseded by black silk (which had become much cheaper), it sold steadily until the 1880s.

However, unquestionably the most successful of the city's products in the 19th century, shawls apart, was 'modern' Norwich crêpe – a new invention designed specifically for mourning and introduced by Joseph Grout in 1822. It was made from twisted silk yarn, woven into very fine gauze, which was dyed black, stiffened with shellac, and finally embossed with characteristic patterns by means of a special and, at first secret, crimping machine. This type of crêpe was the quintessential expression of Victorian grief, lavishly ruched on gowns, hats and bonnets, in amounts dictated by the rigid rituals of mourning etiquette. It was made in Norwich in enormous quantities. Grout's crêpe-making factory (later Grout, Ringer, Martin & Co.) was said to be

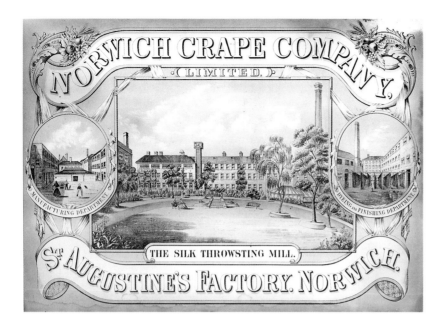

the largest establishment of its kind in the country. Soon there were other Norwich producers, notably Francis Hinde and the Norwich Crape Company. Grout eventually owned several steam-powered silk mills in East Anglia, supplying not only his own works and other crêpe manufacturers, but also the makers of shawls, and silk, or silk-and-worsted fabrics. For a time, mulberry trees planted in the environs of the city provided food for a growing population of silkworms.

Norwich manufacturers might have been better able to recover their lost foreign trade if they had been less reluctant to follow the example of Yorkshire and invest in cost-cutting machinery. The lack of it placed the industry at an enormous competitive disadvantage. Power-spinning of worsted yarn was well established in the Bradford area by 1800, but it was not until 1833 that it was contemplated in Norwich and efforts made to raise the necessary capital. (It is ironic that, in 1818, the bulk of yarn used by Norwich manufacturers was power-spun in Bradford.) At long last, the Albion Mills in King Street, Norwich, were opened in 1837 for the spinning of yarn, and in 1836 building was begun in the St Edmunds and St James parishes of two factories for yarn spinning and for weaving respectively, although they did not go into

production until three years later. The St James building, in particular, was a massive affair, with steam-power, and six floors for hire to individual manufacturers supplying their own machinery. But it was already too late and the factory never worked to full capacity.

At first the power-looms were used only for weaving the simpler fabrics. This underlines one of the industry's great difficulties. Many of the city's high-class and complex products did not lend themselves to mechanical processing, and even after the introduction of power-weaving, handloom-weaving continued to be as important as ever. Norwich in the 19th century was, as it had always been, the proud centre of a luxury trade, and the industry refused to be pushed downmarket by competition from the North.

It is easy to be critical of the apparent lethargy and lack of enterprise that delayed the progress of the Industrial Revolution in Norwich. But conditions in the city were in many ways exceptional. East Anglia lacked fast-running streams that could have provided water-power in the initial stages of mechanisation, and it was far removed from sources of iron and coal. More importantly, it was distant from the centre of developing textile technology in the north-east.

These physical constraints, however, were probably of less moment than the human factor. The close-knit and introverted character of the industry encouraged the growth of a corporate radicalism, which led all too often to militancy and to unruly behaviour. The city's workers had a well-earned reputation for organised rioting and violence.

In 1790, before England was drawn into the French Wars and trade was still booming, wage-rates were fixed by agreement between the manufacturers and weavers, and scales of payment for all the different types of product were posted up in the workplaces. This arrangement remained in force for some years, firmly insisted upon by an intransigent Weavers' Committee whatever the conditions of trade. Any suggestion that wage-rates should be reduced to increase the competitiveness of the city's products was met with strikes and threats of violence. The consequent over-supply of labour made manufacturers hesitant to contemplate the introduction of machinery.

The period between 1826 and 1830 was particularly difficult, with patchy orders and a slump in bombazine manufacture. Two bombazine firms became insolvent in 1829, one of them the old-established family business of Martineau. Indeed, this was a crisis year. Norwich weavers were infuriated by rumours that their employers were sending work into the country and paying lower rates. Towards the end of the year manufacturers broached yet again the dangerous question of selective reductions in wages, backed by the well-meaning, but perhaps misguided, Court of Guardians, whose members were much concerned that Poor Law payments were climbing beyond available resources. A few manufacturers supported the weavers, conscious that their workers faced stretches of unemployment and a precarious livelihood. A series of acrimonious meetings followed, with the weavers becoming more and more belligerent. Finally, the ringleaders marched to the house of the unfortunate Chairman of the Court of Guardians, shouting abuse, determined on violence. After his gates had been pulled down, and windows broken, the 7th Dragoon Guards were called in to quell the riot.

There could hardly have been a worse time to consider introducing the power-looms which were already widespread in Lancashire and the West Riding. No manufacturer would be prepared to risk capital, and indeed, his personal safety, in such circumstances. As a newspaper commentator pointed out, if machinery was set up, it would most likely be broken. Nevertheless, technical progress could not be held back for ever, and in 1836 the building of factories for spinning and weaving was at last undertaken. Understandably, the situation in the industry continued to be turbulent, with further strikes and rioting in 1838. There is no doubt that during this difficult period the city's textile workers endured severe hardship and misery.

By the middle of the century trade had revived to some extent, but it was much reduced in volume, and only a handful of manufacturers remained. Moreover, the revival, such as it was, was short-lived. In the final decline of the industry, changes of fashion played their part, as they had done so often before. Shawls were little worn after the 1870s as female fancy turned from the crinoline to the bustle. But, perhaps an even greater catastrophe, the demand for Norwich crêpe waned rapidly after the formation, in 1875, of the National Mourning Reform Association, a symptom of the final rebellion of Victorian society against the expensive and dreary rituals of grief.

It is difficult to see the decline of the Norwich industry as 'decay', as some have called it. The inventiveness and skills of its workers were undiminished, and the products of the 19th century, whether machine- or hand-made, were as technically accomplished and well-designed as ever. Unfortunately, they were overtaken, like so many other things, by the whims of fashion, and mass-production.

I would like to record my grateful thanks to the staff of the Local Studies Library, Norwich Central Library, for their willing help, to David Cubitt for passing on to me many useful extracts from the Norwich newspapers, and to Dr R G Wilson, Director of the Centre of East Anglian Studies, University of East Anglia, for his valuable suggestions and comments on the text.

2 The First Fifteen Years of the Norwich Shawl Industry
1785–1800

PAMELA CLABBURN

The city of Norwich in the 18th century was first and foremost a city of textile manufacturers and workers. The heads of the firms were influential men, who held office as Mayor or Sheriff, were Aldermen or on the City Council. At the time there was no factory system and the weavers worked at home, taking their webs, when finished, back to the warehouse, and collecting fresh yarn for more work.

The fabrics they were weaving were lightweight worsteds or even lighter 'half-silks', that is, fabrics of mixed yarns with a silk warp and a wool weft, suitable for ladies' wear. These were fashion fabrics and, as in all industries pertaining to fashion, very much at the mercy of the whims and caprices of women who were always wanting change.

Far from England and Norwich was Kashmir, a mountainous country north of India, where there had been for long a tradition of weaving fabric from the fine soft fleece of the mountain goat (*Capra hircus*). As with all animals, the fleece became thicker and finer the higher the altitude and these wild goats living high in the Himalayas were no exception. The finest part of their wool was from the underbelly, and every spring this was shed onto bushes and twigs from which it was picked by the natives. It was washed, spun, dyed and woven into shawls, worn mostly by men as sashes and plaids, but also by women in cold weather, put over the head and thrown over one shoulder. Because of the scarcity of this wool and the method of weaving, the shawls were rare, expensive and in general used as presents from one potentate to another.

In Kashmir weaving was done by the time-consuming tapestry-twill method. This approximates to the European method of weaving tapestries, the difference being that whereas with the tapestries the weave was tabby (the weft threads pass over and under each warp thread), in India the weave was twill (the weft threads pass over two or three warp threads at a time, giving a distinctive diagonal line). As in tapestry weaving, each colour was put in with a separate shuttle (see chapter 6 on weaving techniques). This method, while giving excellent results, is extremely time-consuming and a shawl could take up to eighteen months to weave.

In Kashmir many of the weavers were of Persian origin and the motif most generally used, however much changed, was the Persian or Indian motif known as the *buta* or *boteh* which was originally a graceful flower complete with roots not unlike the Elizabethan embroidered slips. This motif gradually changed into something more like a vase of flowers, or a bunch of flowers tied at the stems. As time went on the flower heads became tighter, the vase disappeared and the shape changed a little with the tip of the plant turning over at the top. This was the design which swept Europe in the late 18th and 19th century.

These Indian shawls made an instant appeal to the manufacturers of the city, who felt that their expertise in the weaving of lightweight fabrics would translate admirably into the weaving of these beautiful garments.

The first that is known definitely about the trade in Norwich is given in a letter written by Alderman John Harvey, a textile manufacturer, to Mr More, the Secretary of the Society of Arts, on 15 March 1788. The Society had awarded a silver medal to Miss Ann Ives of Spalding for very fine

A token issued by Alderman John Harvey of Norwich, in 1792. The reverse shows a weaver at his loom, while the *obverse carries a representation of the city arms, the lion and castle, with the date. The drawing of the* *18th-century loom shows it to be a very rough-and-ready affair and also shows why looms rate such little money in* *inventories. Often they were owned by the manufacturer and hired out to the weaver, to be used by him in his home.*
CASTLE MUSEUM, NORWICH

spinning, so fine that no manufacturer could be found to weave it except Mr Harvey of Norwich. He had been asked to try by Sir Joseph Banks. In his letter to Mr More, Alderman Harvey, referring to the sheep's wool being spun by Miss Ives, says:

> . . . yarn spun so very light . . . from so coarse a material, is rather curious than useful; for though it would make stuff very thin and fine, it would not be sufficiently soft and silky. It equals, in fineness of thread, the yarn of which the India shawls are made, but it bears no comparison to its softness and silkiness . . . In a manufactory of shawls which I have invented, my constant endeavour has been to procure wool sufficiently soft. (*Transactions of the Society of Arts*, vol. VII)

This, for many years, was the main problem for the young shawl industry and for the most part it was overcome by using a combination of wool and silk – silk for strength in the warp and wool for the weft.

From Alderman Harvey's letter it is clear that

he had had the idea of weaving shawls for some time and it is interesting to speculate what would have happened if he had not had working for him a man called Philip John Knights.

What we know of P J Knights is mostly what he tells us himself in advertisements and what we can read about him in the local newspapers. He does not appear in the poll-tax books but there was a Henry Knight, who may be his father, living in Colegate at the time. We do not know in what capacity Knights worked for Alderman Harvey, whether as weaver or designer – probably the latter – or when he struck out on his own. What we do know is that by 1792 he had discovered how to weave 'a shawl counterpane, 4 yds square, manufactured by him; which on examination appeared to be of greater breadth than any goods of equal fineness and texture, hitherto produced to the Society [of Arts] or to their knowledge woven in the Kingdom' (*ibid.*).

In July 1792, P J Knights was, like Miss Ann Ives before him, awarded the Silver Medal of the Society of Arts for this counterpane. It had no seams and was in imitation of the East India shawl counterpanes. Mr Hemming of London, who presented the counterpane to the Society, says in a letter that:

> He [Mr Knights] has brought the manufacture to so great a perfection in shawls, waistcoat shapes etc. that they can hardly be distinguished from the Indian, though they can be afforded at one-twentieth of the price usually given for the same articles which are brought from India. I understand that the largest articles ever attempted to be made in this country, prior to the one now presented, are only one and a half yards wide. (*ibid.*)

From this letter, and a further one written by P J Knights to the Society in 1792, it is clear that there must be a distinction made between the item, a shawl, and the fabric, generally at this date known as shawling. Shawling could be, and was, made into different articles of dress, both male and female, such as ladies' train dresses and men's waistcoat shapes as well as counterpanes and long scarfs. The fabric was always woven a plain off-white, and then the design, instead of being woven in, as was done later, was embroidered in a darning stitch, generally by children.

In another letter to the Society P J Knights explains that the counterpane

> cannot be retailed at a price less than £20, to be 16 quarters square, as it is; and £15 if 12 quarters, embroidered in the same manner: if plain, with a fringe only, it will come up at 8 guineas, 16 quarters; and 6 guineas, if 12 quarters fringed. Please to observe, the middle being left plain, it is intended for the coat of arms of the purchaser, to be embroidered in, if they please, and at their own expense, by sending down the drawing and size. (*ibid.*)

There are, so far as is known, only two of these counterpanes in existence. One is in Strangers Hall Museum, Norwich (cat. no. 74) and is the prototype of the counterpane sent by Mr Knights to Queen Charlotte in 1792. It is exactly as stated in

Mr Knights' letter, 16 quarters square, with a silk warp and wool weft, and a silk fringe. In the centre are embroidered (in darning stitch) the Arms of England, round the edge is a design of roses, daffodils and shamrocks, and in the four corners are representations of the Garter.

An embroidered bunch of flowers from the border of the 1793 shawl counterpane at Blickling Hall, Norfolk. The motif pre-dates the more exactly composed pine-shaped designs seen in the later woven shawls. The embroidery is entirely worked in darning stitch and would have been done by children such as The Little Norwich-Shawl Worker. NATIONAL TRUST, BLICKLING HALL, NORFOLK

The other counterpane, sadly, has been cut up, but is on view as part of the bed in the Chinese bedroom at Blickling Hall. The bedhead has the Hobart arms as the centrepiece and the border has been pleated to form the valance to the bed.

This border shows, alternately, the shield of various families possibly connected with the Hobarts, and bunches of tightly massed flowers, tied at the base with a small ribbon. The bunches are obviously copied or adapted from those seen on the Indian shawls. There are also, though not on the bed, four representations of the Hobart bull which would have been in the four corners. Clearly a counterpane of the £20 calibre.

From July 1792, P J Knights became more and more prominent in the manufacturing world. The gift of the shawl counterpane to Queen Charlotte led to his appointment as Shawlman to Her Majesty, and he was ordered to make shawls for the Queen and Princesses, not to his own design, but to designs sent down from Windsor. The *Norwich Mercury* of 15 December 1792 recorded that 'Her Majesty and all the Princesses appeared in Norwich Shawl Dresses of Mr Knights' manufacture'.

By September 1793 Knights seems to have taken over from Alderman Harvey and is advertising from his manufactory at 2 Colegate (the Harvey house) and his wholesale warehouse at 11 King Street, Cheapside, London. He was then making and selling Train Dresses, Scarfs, Shawls, Ladies Habit and Gentlemen's Waistcoat Shapes and Riding Cravats.

In the spring of 1793 Knights mounted a very grand show, called the Norwich Shawl Manufactory Exhibition, at 136 New Bond Street, London, which was attended by royalty and many of the nobility. In 1794, in honour of Her Majesty's Birthday, a wonderful display was on view at 'Knights Norwich Shawl Manufactory, Strand', where 'in front of the house was formed a pyramid of lamps; at the windows were seen little children embroidering shawls under festoons of white and gold; and in the centre was placed a beautiful model of a State Bed . . . ' (*Norwich Mercury*, 25 January 1794). He also acted as an agent for

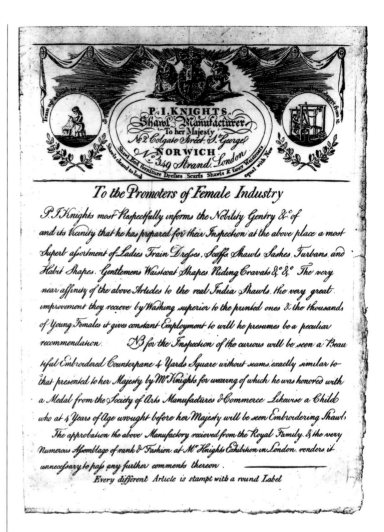

Advertisement circular issued by P J Knights in c.1792. While it publicised his wares, particularly the shawl counterpane, it is worded to appeal to those ladies interested in work for poor women and children.
STRANGERS HALL MUSEUM, NORWICH

other craftsmen and the Duke of Norfolk visited his exhibition and 'assured Mr Knights that he should furnish three new rooms in Arundel Castle with shawl manufacture and expressed it as his particular wish that every part of the furniture should be executed in Norfolk, desiring Mr Knights to find every part of it complete, viz. cabinet work, carving and guilding, upholstery etc.' (*Norfolk Chronicle*, 18 May 1793).

It is obvious that by this time P J Knights had carved out a very successful career for himself.

However, the relationship between him and Harvey can only be surmised – Harvey is never mentioned in connection with the London displays, nor is it clear why in London Knights moved from place to place. There was still some connection with Harvey, as in 1797 Prince William of Gloucester 'ordered a shawl dress of Mr Knights and was much pleased with the royal shawl counterpane in Alderman John Harvey's factory' (*Norwich Mercury*, 22 April 1797). In Norwich Knights' shawl warehouse was now at No. 4 Market Place where for winter he was advertising 'Norwich Shawl Furred Cloaks, Shawl, Furr Dresses and Waistcoat Pieces, trimmed with the much approved blue furr and other furrs [*sic*] of the newest fashion.'

Trevor Fawcett shows that in 1795 Knights opened a shop in the most fashionable street in Bath, Milsom Street, where he shared the premises with a firm of muslin manufacturers from Glasgow (*Norfolk Archaeology* XLI (1), 1990, p 67). There, in 1797, he showed the same wares as were showing in Norwich and London, i.e., 'an Elegant Assortment of Ladies' Train Dresses, Scarfs, Shawls, Sashes, Cravats and Gentleman's Waistcoats'. The square shawls, embroidered, still by hand, sold for 4 to 6 guineas. In 1798 he added Turbans, Habit Shapes and Riding Cravats to his stock, but by 1800 he had ceased to advertise and closed his shop at Bath. He, surprisingly at this date, had dresses made up in London, from his shawling, to sell ready-made: 'He has just received from the first Mantua and Trimming Warehouse in London a most elegant assortment of his manufactured Train Dresses completely made up and trimmed . . . ' (*Norfolk Chronicle*, 25 January 1794). At this time, though ready-made dresses were obtainable for the poor, it was seldom that first-class dresses were ever other than bespoke.

In 1794 P J Knights advertised in the *Norwich Mercury* that while he was still manufacturing at 2 Colegate, his warehouse would be at 4 Gentlemans Walk, a much better venue for high-class sales. His prices appear reasonable, and were certainly much less than for the Indian equivalent: Train Dresses for 2 to 10 guineas; Embroidered Long Scarfs 18 shillings to 6 guineas; Embroidered Shawls 10 shillings to 6 guineas; and Plain Shawls 7s. 6d. to 1 guinea. For the winter he was also selling Shawl Cloaks.

In 1803 he had acquired some cashmere yarn, 'the same material from which the real Indian Shawls are made', and there is a comparable small advertisement in 1804 – but thereafter all is silence. What happened? We do not know. He was made Sheriff of the city in 1809 and died at Greenwich on 24 April 1833. We have no further information on him.

While P J Knights is the shawl manufacturer of the late 1700s of whom we know the most – due to his great capacity for self-promotion, his undoubted ability in inventing new product lines and his obvious skill in manufacturing – he was by no means the only shawl maker of that time. By 1800 there appear in the Norwich directory the names of twenty manufacturers, mostly noted just as 'shawl maker', several with 'cotton' added (probably referring to the trade in muslin shawls then being made) and two also making bombazine and crêpe. About these men we know little or nothing, but about one manufacturer, whose name does not appear in the directories, we know rather more.

His name was Richard Bidwell and he was a sack manufacturer and also the godson of John Jarrold I, a draper at Woodbridge in Suffolk, and a very astute businessman. In 1795 the two men entered into partnership. The agreement states that 'R Bidwell and John Jarrold agree to enter to co-partnership in the Shawl, Scarf and Waistcoat Shapes Trade . . . ', obviously still selling shawls and shawling side by side (Jarrold family archives). Although they agreed to put equal shares of money into the business, Jarrold paid Bidwell 15 guineas a year as the latter was the active partner while Jarrold merely kept a very strict eye on the business. He was the senior partner and Bidwell was somewhat in awe of him.

In the same year there is a list of the 'utensils' Bidwell put into the partnership. This included one loom, also a print board and trestles, and the most expensive item, printing blocks charged at

£9. 16s. 6d. There is no reference anywhere to shawls being printed at this time, so it is likely that the blocks were used to outline the designs for the embroiderers to follow. The firm sold shawls to Manchester, Huddersfield and Halifax and in one parcel which is itemised they are all ⁶/₄ size, i.e., 1½ yards square, all embroidered, ranging in price from 7 shillings to 9 shillings each. This particular parcel sent to Messrs Buzzard & Co of Manchester in 1798 contained eight dozen shawls. Although a small firm, they appear to have done very well in the late 1700s. In 1796 Bidwell wrote to Jarrold: 'Our Shawl trade is wonderfully brisk. Have now 18 looms at work and could employ without exaggeration 3 or 4 times as many.' At this date they were making Scarfs, Scarf Cloaks, Undress Shawls and Common Shawls (all embroidered), White Scarfs, Embroidered Rich Scarfs, Bordered and Cornered Scarfs, Waistcoat Shapes, Shawl Dress Shapes, Stripe Shapes, Embroidered Shapes and Rough Embroidered Shapes.

The partnership, which like all the trading of this period, had its ups and downs, was not dissolved until 1811.

By the turn of the century the Norwich shawl trade, which still included shawling, had grown to comprise more than twenty manufacturers (not every firm is listed in the trade directories) and was very buoyant, so much so that in 1803 at Norwich Quarter Sessions wages were fixed for the shawl weavers as distinct from weavers of other fabrics. It is also worthy of note that in 1803, in the infant country of Australia, the *Sydney Gazette* lists 'Norwich and Cotton Shawls' at the famous department store of Lords. The industry had moved a long way in a short time.

3 The Norwich Shawl Industry in the Nineteenth Century

PAMELA CLABBURN

The Little Norwich-Shawl Worker, *painted by Joseph Clover in 1815 and engraved by Thomas Overton in 1826, shows a child embroidering a shawl. It is surprising that the picture should have been painted at such a late date. Shawls were certainly embroidered (darned) by children until about 1800, but by 1815 the method was replaced by the drawloom, which was capable of weaving the fillover patterns. It would seem that Clover was attracted to the subject, and was not necessarily making a truthful record of the times.*
CASTLE MUSEUM, NORWICH

The story of the Norwich shawl industry during the 19th century is punctuated by periods of comparative prosperity, deep recessions and the intransigence of the Norwich weaver together with his deep aversion to new methods. As most of the information which can be gleaned about the industry in this period comes from reports in the local newspapers, it is difficult to get a balanced picture, as news generally had to be bad to be reported, and periods of calm and affluence are seldom mentioned.

It is clear, however, that by the first decade of the century shawls had come to stay. They were new, colourful and warm, attributes much appreciated by ladies in a period when fashion decreed mainly white or very light colours and flimsy fabrics. Warm and colourful shawls were a godsend.

More and more manufacturers turned to weaving shawls, in addition to their usual fabrics, and shawl manufacture was affected by the economic ups and downs of the times. The early years of the century were successful and on 21 January 1804 the *Norwich Mercury* could state with pride that: 'Norwich manufactured shawls are in such high repute that one manufacturer in the city has received an order for not less that 42,000. Such an order must necessarily give employment to a great number of men, women and children.'

The problems involved in trying to make shawls feel as if they were made with the fine soft goat wool from Kashmir – which was virtually unobtainable in Europe except in minute quantities – continued. Many compromises were tried both in France and England: goats were brought from

16

Kashmir but did not do well, and other wools were tried. One landowner who was very interested and anxious to help was the great agriculturalist Mr Coke of Holkham. His yearly shearings were famous and anyone interested was welcome. In both 1806 and 1807 shawls were shown there made by two manufacturers, John Herring and Thomas Paul, from 'the wool of Mr Coke's Southdown Sheep'. John Herring also mixed Southdown wool with merino. Thomas Paul tried merino alone – but it was found that the Southdown wool was the more economical. Wool from Mr Tollett's Spanish shearlings was also tried but was found not to be suitable for shawl making. In the end silk and sometimes cotton was used for the warps and wool for the wefts. From the shawls in the collection it is clear that for the next twenty or thirty years various types and combinations of wool and silk were tried; some shawls are harsh to the feel, while some are heavy, some soft and some light in weight.

In 1807 the shawl manufacturers had a clash with the Board of Trade. Shawls at this time could be rather more than a yard square or could be long and narrow. The Customs and Excise officers decided that if a shawl was more than 1 yard square it ceased to be a 'handkerchief' and became a 'garment', and so was subject to extra duty. The shawl manufacturers and printers appealed to Mr Patteson and Mr Smith, the Norwich MPs, who took up their case with the Rt Hon George Rose, Vice President of the Board of Trade. The *Norwich Mercury* of 5 September reports with restrained glee that: 'Mr Rose saw the reasonableness of the complaint and promised every assistance in his power to obtain relief for the shawl manufacturers and printers.' In consequence the statute was rescinded and Mr Smith was rewarded with a piece of plate valued at 100 guineas. What was given to Mr Patteson is not recorded.

In 1809 trade was still going well and the manufacturers decided to increase the wages of the weavers – not before time, as it was stated that a man with a family, working twelve to fourteen hours a day, found it impossible to live without parish relief. This was the last time wages were raised for many years.

The wars with France ended in 1815, but England had had many years of war, and was in no state to counter the fact that restrictions on imports were relaxed. Trade was bad and troubles began. In various published letters in 1822 the masters said that Yorkshire goods were cheaper, and that, in order to compete, both prices and wages must come down. This was not merely a Norwich problem, but was happening all over England, so much so that at a meeting of wool combers and weavers in Norwich it was agreed to start a subscription for the working poor of Bradford. By 1826 things had got so bad that at a meeting for the Relief of the Poor it was said that only approximately one third of the looms in the city were working and that only 18 out of 42 families had work. In the *Norwich Mercury* of 20 September 1826 one letter made the point that the present difficulties were largely due to the fact that when times were good too many people with too little experience had jumped on the bandwagon: 'Many shopkeepers whose capital was barely sufficient to enable them to conduct their business adequately, elated with the idea of being manufacturers, directed capital and attention from one business which they understood, to another of which they were ignorant.'

By 1827 prices had reached rock bottom and the retailer Wm Eastwood was advertising in the *Norwich Mercury* '10,000 real silk Norwich shawls in small size 2/3 each and full two yards square from 6/- to 15/-'.

The 1830s were noticeable for the gradual resurgence of the trade and the production of some of the most beautiful shawls made in Norwich. It is a matter of individual taste as to which period produced the most charming shawls, but certainly the 1830s and 1840s must be among the best both in technique and design. This was largely due to the firm of Towler, Campin & Co., a firm over which Abel Towler presided for many years, though he changed partners with great regularity. But however many different partners he had, he always had weavers working for him to the highest standards.

There must have been many other firms with not such high standards as great alarm was felt over the poor designs which were being turned out. In competition with France, Norwich, as well as Paisley, was at a disadvantage. For many years France had had schools of design which were geared to the needs of manufacturers, with the result that firms in both England and Scotland frequently looked to France for their designs. An entry in the accounts of Grout & Co. for 1834, for example, reads: '6 French handkerchiefs bought for patterns, £1'; and other manufacturers either went to France themselves or sent one of their employees to collect designs for use in England. The Government of the day felt that better training was needed in England and, in 1842, Schools of Design were opened in various cities, including Norwich. Sadly these schools did not fulfil their obligations. Instead of encouraging design for commerce they insisted on strict training in drawing from the antique, which was not helpful to shawl design. In 1849 Mr Poynter, H M Inspector, writes sadly that:

> When the Norwich School was established there seemed to be some promise of a direct benefit to the shawl manufacture, the only one of the staple trades of the town admitting much scope for design . . . The prospect has not improved and such little connexion as there was between the manufacture and the school has nearly ceased . . . (quoted in Marjorie Allthorpe, *A Happy Eye: A School of Art in Norwich, 1845–1982*, 1982)

However, in 1850 Mr Poynter was pleased to write:

> It is gratifying to state that one of the shawl manufacturers [probably Blakeley] has at length selected a pupil from the school to assist his designer and that he has made application for another . . . It is the first example which has occurred of this mode of connexion between the School and the manufactory. (*ibid.*)

Not a great result after eight years of training.

In 1850 there was an Exhibition of Modern Manufacture at the Society of Arts and the *Journal of Design and Manufacturers* reviewed the fabrics. One of the remarks must have been endorsed by many people, both at that date and later. The critic said: 'In Norwich shawls the introduction of gold thread into the weaving has been successfully attempted by Messrs Blakeley. We much wish, however, notwithstanding the acknowledged excellence of the Indian patterns, that the Indian principle were occasionally adopted to other forms instead of the eternal pine'. This pious hope was not to be. People wanted the pine and the pine they got – by this date not in isolated beauty, but in so many writhings and convolutions that all form disappeared.

As a result of the disastrous depression of the 1820s, not only was the School of Design started, but also, in 1838, a Commission was appointed by the Government to enquire into the plight of the handloom weavers. The Commission published its findings, *A Commission to Report on the Conditions of the Hand-loom Weavers*, in 1839. Mr Mitchell, the Commissioner, took evidence from weavers as well as manufacturers. William Stark, the dyer, told of the time consumed in preparing a loom for a new pattern and pointed out that a weaver was only paid for what he wove, and not for the time spent in preparing the loom. Because a shawl was a fashion garment, the designs had to be changed frequently and so if a weaver set up a loom for a certain design he could only expect to weave one or two before changing the design, with more loss of time.

The caprice of fashion was one of the major problems of the trade, and it was emphasised by Mr Etheridge in the Report. He was complaining, like Mr Stark, of the time it took to set up a loom and said that: 'he had brought out a shawl of a most beautiful pattern and it was taking well and yielding a good profit; but he had just received a letter from his London agent, telling him that his pattern had been imitated by the Scotch, and advising him to discontinue it immediately'. (*A Commission to Report*). He added: 'When the Scotch take up a pattern they inundate the market with such an abundance that the article becomes quite common and ladies of property will not buy a shawl of which there are so many imitations' (*ibid.*).

This 'piracy', as it was called, led to the protection of patterns and designs as Mr Etheridge had wanted, and from 1842 it became possible to register designs at the Public Record Office, in some cases for three, and in others for six, months. The fee for each registration was 1 shilling and, in view of the protection it gave to both manufacturer and weaver at such low cost, it is surprising that so little use was made of it. Of all the manufacturers in Norwich between 1842 and 1875, a mere seven firms availed themselves of the opportunity, and one can only wonder why the others did not. The very moderate fee should not have been a burden and it does seem possible that the manufacturers had been 'crying wolf', and that perhaps piracy was not as rife as they made out. However, Strangers Hall Museum is happy that even those seven found it worth their while, as it means that there are in the Public Record Office 315 designs, both woven and printed, against which shawls can be checked and which give an excellent guide to patterns fashionable at certain dates. It is also interesting to note that designs did not have to be used in their entirety for the protection to apply. The 1-shilling fee could go a long way.

Among other things, the Report gave a comprehensive tally of the number of weavers in the city. It said that in 1839 there were 4,054 handlooms working (therefore the same number of weavers), of which 3,398 were in the houses of weavers and 656 in shops and factories. Of the 4,054 total, 387 weavers were producing silk and fillover shawls but only 30 were working Jacquard looms. Although the report does not make it clear which weavers were working the Jacquards, it

seems that the shawl weavers always preferred the drawloom. Of all the shawls in the Museum only one firm, that of Clabburn, Sons & Crisp, appears to have used the Jacquard extensively, and then not until the 1850s. Whether this was a question of workers' intransigence or the lack of new machinery which was always being cited as one of the main problems of the Norwich trade, it is difficult to say. Probably it was a mixture of both. There is no doubt that the Norwich weaver was a most difficult workman. He was independent, pig-headed and, for the time, well educated. Most

An engraving showing the two parts of the manufactory of Willett & Nephew. Above: the house in Pottergate, Norwich, where his drawloom weavers, who worked at home, brought their finished work and collected their pay and fresh yarn for the next job, be it shawl or fabric. Below: the floor in St James Factory which the firm hired for those who worked the steam-power machines. St James Factory was let out floor by floor to any manufacturer who needed power-looms. In the 1820s Willett tried to modernise the shawl industry and introduced power-looms and Jacquard looms, but in so doing incurred the wrath of the weavers, who feared the loss of their jobs.
BRIDEWELL MUSEUM, NORWICH

journeymen, at all events, could read and write and the conditions under which they worked, where they were free to work the hours they wished as long as they got the work done, made it possible for them to take the odd few minutes off, when they could have a smoke and discuss the issues of the day with their neighbour.

The Report goes on to say that of the shawl weavers 250 worked in private houses and 137 in shops or factories. The largest factory had 149 looms in one shop.

The only concrete effects of the Commission seem to have been the setting-up of the School of Design, and the opportunity for the manufacturers to register their designs.

In 1842 there was another weavers' strike in the city, and again it was over wages, with the weavers standing out for the wages they had had eighteen months before which had since been reduced. The manufacturers again said that they could not afford to pay more than was paid in Paisley, that Norwich still suffered from Paisley piracy, that there was no prospect of an increase in trade and, in short, that they had no intention of paying more. So there were large meetings on Castle Meadow of the handloom weavers and on Chapel Field of the Jacquard weavers and eventually the strike was abandoned.

During the later part of the 1840s the large manufacturers were working towards the Great Exhibition of 1851, but as always there were reports in the newspapers on the state of the poor. In 1849, the *Norfolk Chronicle* and *Norwich Gazette* sent a reporter round to the homes of some of the working classes, to find out exactly what their lives were like, and they felt that one anecdote was worth reporting. It concerns Jenny Lind, the 'Swedish Nightingale', who was very fond of Norwich and sang here as often as she could. The reporter was told to go to the home of a weaver in Silver Road, who was supposed to be one of the best workers and had made a shawl to be given as a present to Jenny Lind. He told the reporter that it took him five weeks to prepare the loom for the shawl. The pattern took well and he was employed for three-quarters of the year in making other

shawls of the same pattern. He could make about one a week, and was paid 24s. 10d. each for making them. Out of that he had to pay the winder 2s. 6d., the hire of the loom was 2s. 6d., a drawboy 7s., 'picking' 6d., and at night he needed three candles at 4d. each. His expenses therefore were 13s. 6d. which left clear 11s. 4d. for his week's work. He said Miss Lind was very kind and sent round to ask him if he needed anything. He said he wanted nothing as 'I thought it would be imposing like upon her', but she insisted that he must have something so his daughter suggested that he needed a greatcoat. Miss Lind sent a tailor to measure him, and she paid the cost and ' "I hadn't had one for many years before that." Miss Lind did a world of good for the poor weavers when she was here, and they all adored her for it.' (*Norfolk Chronicle* and *Norwich Gazette*, 29 December 1849).

The Great Exhibition of 1851 gave the Norwich manufacturers a wonderful opportunity to show their wares to a great number of people, especially those from overseas. Again, few firms entered shawls, or possibly more entered but their goods were turned down. However, those who were represented produced shawls of excellent quality. Queen Victoria noted in her diary of 14 June: 'Went first through one or two of the French Courts and then upstairs to examine in detail the Norwich shawls, of the lightest Cashmir material, also of silk with beautiful designs . . . '.

Later in 1855 Her Majesty bought two shawls from Clabburn, Sons & Crisp, facsimiles of those which had been entered in the Exposition of the French Palais de l'Industrie. The jury of the exhibition had voted a gold medal to the firm, but when the decision came before the Royal Commission they decided to award the large silver medal because, 'looking to the character of Norwich as a manufacturing city, its manufacturers (except Clabburn) had contributed nothing directly to the Exposition'. As can be imagined the city of Norwich was incensed at the French unfairness.

One of the difficulties in the graceful wearing of a shawl was the fact that it had a right and a wrong side. This meant that if the wind blew or the shawl had not been perfectly arranged the wrong side would show. India had overcome the problem by weaving shawls in pairs which were worn back to back, but their shawls were lighter in weight, so it was possible to wear two at once. The small turnover shawl of the 1820s had managed by sewing on two of the borders in reverse, so that when the shawl was folded diagonally the two smaller borders appeared above the two larger on the back of the wearer, creating a most attractive design. With the bigger and heavier shawls of the 1850s and 1860s, it became more difficult to manage the garment with elegance. The answer seemed to be a reversible shawl, and Paisley was the first centre to produce an acceptable type, as early as 1845. This was followed in 1854 by what the newspapers referred to as the Norwich New Silk Persian Shawl or the Persian Silk Ling Shawl. The *Norwich Mercury* extolled its virtues and said that it would not cost more than £5, would be 4 yards long, 2 yards wide and would weigh under 2 pounds. It was developed by Clabburn, Sons & Crisp but unfortunately there is no specimen in the

Museum, neither have we seen one. It seems that the firm of C & F Bolingbroke & Jones made some, however, as in the collection is a double-sided shawl made by the weaver William Armes of Barrack Street (cat. no. 127). He is remembered as taking his beam, to have his web cut off, to a firm in St Clements Alley. The only firm in that alley at this date was C & F Bolingbroke & Jones, so it is likely that they also made reversible shawls.

In spite of the success of the reversible shawl, the need for shawls was gradually dying out. Even in the 1850s there were not so many looms as in the previous decade, and in the 1860s there were even fewer. The marriage of the beautiful Alexandra of Denmark to Edward, Prince of Wales, gave the textile industry a fillip, and both the Crape Company and Clabburn, Sons & Crisp gave the bride shawls as presents from the city, the latter company giving what were known as their Patent Shawls.

But by the end of the 1860s the shawl trade was dying. It is noticeable that the registered designs of Clabburn, Sons & Crisp, the last firm to register,

Both in France and Britain shawls can occasionally be found which have a circular trademark sewn on. They are always beautifully woven and it appears that they were only sewn on to very special shawls; in fact Strangers Hall Museum has only two, this one and another referring to the retailer Caley's as 'Shawlman to Her Majesty'.
STRANGERS HALL MUSEUM, NORWICH

21

incidentally, were all for furnishing fabrics. In fact, in some of their later shawls in the collection the designs are such that they were probably used for furnishing as well as for shawls.

The decline of the trade was not surprising: women had been wearing shawls for nearly a hundred years and wanted a change. The growing preference for bustles rather than the wide crinolines precluded the graceful hang of the shawl, and the final blow was the Franco-Prussian War which was the death-knell of the shawl in France and Britain as well.

The Sunday School, *by Robert McInnes. This painting of the early 1850s shows that by this date shawls had become normal wear for children as well as adults. The children are all well-clothed and shod, but the wearing of this type of shawl makes them look rather elderly.*
PAISLEY MUSEUM AND ART GALLERIES

4 *The Social Background to the Shawl*

PENELOPE ALFREY

. . . the chief item in this inventory, the spell by which she struck a certain awe through the household, quelling the otherwise scornfully disposed teachers and servants, and, so long as her broad shoulders wore the folds of that majestic drapery, even influencing madame herself – a real Indian shawl – 'un véritable Cachmire', as Madame Beck said, with mixed reverence and amaze. I feel quite sure that without this 'Cashmire' she would not have kept her footing in the pensionnat for two days; by virtue of it, and it only, she maintained the same a month.

(Charlotte Brontë, Villette, 1853, p 133)

It does not require a knowledge of 19th-century fashions to realise, in this telling extract from *Villette*, that Brontë was aware of the extraordinary influence that the shawl could command. Through its power to transform its wearer, a power that could override other, conflicting, evidence of status, the shawl bestowed respectability. As this passage indicates, the awe and respect that it attracted was slow to be challenged. Flaunted and treasured by those who had it, the shawl was coveted and revered, and fostered envy amongst those who lacked it.

More than a passing high fashion, the shawl continued to be worn throughout the 19th century as an enduring emblem of femininity. Its descent from a rare, handcrafted artefact to common, mass-produced imitation has often been regarded as evidence of the economic and technological successes of the shawl industry. However, this series of transitions – from exotic to familiar and commonplace; from expensive to affordable to cheap – also reveals the social currency of the shawl in circulation. The shawl ascended its pinnacle in high fashion during a period of revolution in taste, when aristocratic preference for sensuality, display and exoticism gave way to an increasingly dominant middle-class preference for modesty that shunned ostentation. The range of cultural meanings, concerning both class and gender, that attached to the shawl could explicitly reveal the wearer's social position. Painting, popular prints and literature provide invaluable insight into the interrelationship between femininity and status. Within the limited scope of a short essay, however, evidence of this relationship between the shawl and feminine status is drawn mainly from contemporary literature.

The term 'shawl' relates to a number of types of unstructured lengths of material that were worn around the shoulders, waist and even the head of the wearer. The cashmere shawl, for instance, was a large rectangle of lightweight fabric but, at its height in fashion, the term could also include a scarf (worn around the neck), a veil and a sash, as well as the large square shawl which was the most popular form after the 1830s. The weight and density of weave, pattern and scale would be critical features in determining how, from a considerable range of possibilities, the shawl might be arranged or draped. Thus the term 'shawl' is a generic one that encompasses a great many variations in design, quality, manufacture and arrangement. What is important to note is that, in general terms, the manner in which the shawl was arranged at the beginning of the 19th century is very different to the way it was worn fifty years later. Although this difference can be accounted for by the differentiation in design – that the later shawl was often much larger and heavier, for instance – it also reflects the differences in social attitudes governing the way in which body and clothing were permitted to interact and the subsequent portrayal of women in art and literature.

By the end of the 18th century, when any account of the shawl in high fashion begins, the shawl enjoyed an unrivalled position as an emblem of exoticism and luxury. Such a claim could not be made of any other item of feminine apparel. The key question is, why should a shawl enjoy such focused attention?

In essence, the shawl was nothing more than embellished drapery. Indeed, the cashmere shawl, which was the first fashionable shawl, was admired primarily for its superior draping qualities before purchasers had acquired a taste for its 'strange' surface patterns. In painting, the superior expressive qualities of drapery outrivalled tailored dress and thus had been exploited by fashionable portraitists since the 17th century when the limiting presence of stiff, formal dress in portraiture began to be rejected and a lighter, informal mood began to appear. During the 18th century, fashionable dress absorbed the increasing informality of *déshabillé* and *négligé* effects that were created either by the loose arrangement of draperies or by the contrived escape of unstructured garments that seeped into the formal outer layers of clothing. The introduction of draped muslins that softened the edges – at the neck and wrists – of stiff, unyielding garments hinted at an emerging informality in everyday appearance.

However, certain artists – most notably Joshua Reynolds – had observed that cladding the sitter in a generalised arrangement of fabric which deliberately excluded all reference to contemporary dress conferred the requisite quality of dignity. Thus drapery and dignity became, within artistic circles, synonymous; and both were irreconcilable to the ephemerality of fashionable dress which was

expelled from the more classicised portrait.

Elizabeth Vigée-Lebrun, a leading portrait painter working within the French court until the Revolution, expressed the contempt for contemporary fashion shared by some of her fellow artists and her preference for the unstructured form of classical dress, stressing the role that the shawl prototype played in its promotion:

> [It] was a godsend for painters . . . As I despised the costume then worn by women I tried in every way to make it more picturesque and I was delighted when I obtained the confidence of my sitters who allowed me to drape them as I pleased. Shawls were not then the fashion but I made use of large scarves. In that way I tried to imitate the beautiful draped style of Raphael and Domenichino. (Vigée-Lebrun, *Memoirs*, London, 1989, Letter IV (1775), p 27)

British artists, such as Alan Ramsay or Thomas Gainsborough, who were less concerned with the apparent conflict between fashionable dress and the ideals of the classical world, might incorporate a gauzy scarf, moving with an apparent force of its own, to form a sinuous line in contrast with the ordered, flat surfaces of tailored dress. The harsh lines of dress in the second half of the century were occasionally softened by the addition of the fichu, a softly draped muslin that enveloped the shoulders, framing the décolletage or, conversely, concealing it. The fichu can thus be interpreted as the intermediate stage in the supplanting by soft drapery of the stiff, unyielding surfaces of formal dress. It was also the precursor of that note of ambiguity between display and modesty that the shawl created so effectively by the turn of the century.

Thus the shawl, worn by women in pursuit of fashion and status, was analogous to the role that drapery had played in portraiture. Drapery had entered the world of fashionable dress in the guise of the shawl, to offer both versatility and practicality within the aesthetics of neo-classical taste. What had been an accessory in artistic representation became an essential accessory in everyday dress that defined both what was fashionable and what was dignified, the two elements of appearance that Reynolds in his *Fourth Discourse on Art* (1771) had declared were incompatible.

The value that attached to drapery within aesthetic discourse was not confined to the 18th century but continued well into the 19th. Ruskin in *The Stones of Venice* (1851–3) expressed very similar sentiments to Reynolds when he described drapery in painting as: 'one of the main helps to dignity of character and courtesy of bearing' (*Everyman's Library*, vol. III, undated, p 54). Drapery was seen to enhance the element of nobility in visual representation; the shawl was seen to create an aura of distinction in everyday life.

The shawl's initial development into high fashion is not, however, merely the result of a vigorous impetus within the aesthetic domain, the culmination of a series of artists' whims. On the contrary, there was clearly a delay between the shawl's début into European society and its acceptance as essential wear. It first appeared in England – see, for instance, Sterne's letter of 1767 to Eliza Draper, wife of an East India Company official who had access to the rare supplies of the Indian shawl (L P Curtis (ed), *Letters of Lawrence Sterne*, Oxford, 1935, Letter 193, March 1767). English manufacturers then lost no time in their attempt to produce an imitation, yet it was in France that the shawl established itself as a highly fashionable accessory. Nevertheless, once the shawl became popularised by the French, it rapidly gained ground within English society. The cost and difficulty in obtaining such an item, in England and France, restricted its use to the affluent and aristocratic and those on the fringes of such illustrious circles. 'Over her fair and finely turned shoulders', recorded the Duchesse d'Abrantès of Thérèse Tallien's ultra modish ensemble in 1796, 'was thrown a superb red cachemire shawl, an article at that time very rare and in great request. She disposed it around her in a manner at once graceful and picturesque' (*Memoirs of the Duchesse d'Abrantès*, London, vol. I, 1831–5, p 247).

In appearance the cashmere shawl was unmistakably foreign in colour, pattern and texture, dimensions and even smell, all of which conveyed the opulence and sensuality of eastern culture. Thus it is hardly surprising that when it began to appear in France, 'nobody knew what use to make of them. It was determined that they would make pretty "couvrepieds" and veils for the cradle . . . they did not become vogue until after Napoleon's expedition to Egypt, and that even then they took, in the first instance, but slowly' (Countess of Wilton, *Art as Needlework*, 1840, p 228).

It has been suggested by a number of authors that cashmere shawls were initially used as furnishing accessories, incorporated into furnishing schemes requiring accents of intense colour. However, even when the visual evidence overwhelmingly confirms their use as fashionable apparel, they are frequently shown draped over a chair – as testimony to the recent occupation of the deserted room or, in the case of the portrait, as a colourful adjunct to the sitter – but this would appear to have no part in the permanent interior decorative scheme.

Whilst the shawl was gaining commercial strength it began to acquire a wide range of complex, sometimes conflicting, cultural and stylistic associations: within exoticism, because it originated in India and also because eastern dress was generally unstructured; within classicism because, despite its eastern patterns, it was draped in styles akin to antique dress; within egalitarianism, because it could be worn in the traditional form of the kerchief, *à la paysanne*. It could thus embrace both the familiar and the strange, the contemporary and the historic, the elite and the commonplace.

As the cashmere shawl became exported in larger quantities and good quality imitations became increasingly available, the shawl began to be widely perceived as 'the ultimate endorsement of elegance, the indispensable item of dress for anyone who prided herself on being well turned out' (*Grand Dictionnaire Universel du XIXe Siècle*, Paris, 1867). It was a perception that continued until the 1860s. As the choice of design and price in shawls rapidly diversified, the shawl became an ever more subtle indicator or saboteur of its wearer's claim to gentility and good taste. Thus the class and, some would claim, the character of its wearer could be explicitly defined by the shawl. The less confident might resort to formal demonstrations on shawl draping incorporated into etiquette and deportment classes or avail themselves of the advice proffered in the increasing number of ladies' magazines and periodicals. Many must have been discomforted to come across the following opinion in an 1851 issue of the *Englishwoman's Domestic Magazine* that claimed: 'We scarcely know a truer test of a gentlewoman's taste in dress than her selection of a shawl and her manner of wearing it.'

Although it is the Empress Joséphine who is credited with popularising the shawl, the earliest known visual record of the cashmere shawl worn as an accessory to the simple, classically inspired chemise dress is recorded in David's portrait of the *Marquise de Sorcy de Thélusson* (1790). There it is worn with little artifice and appears to confirm that initially the shawl was appreciated for its practical qualities of warmth and softness. However, it should be noted that the artist was not the least interested in those features that might recommend it to its wearer – it is included in the painting because of its 'picturesque' qualities, not its functional ones. The comments of contemporary observers, such as those of the aforementioned Duchesse d'Abrantès, suggest that the imported Indian shawl was admired and valued primarily for its striking aesthetic qualities, not its practical ones.

In 1793, a Kashmir-style shawl (but in a very unusual colour) appears in the portrait of *Lady*

Burdett by Thomas Lawrence. If the shawl was initially popularised by the French, the date of this work would suggest that the English were not slow to follow suit.

The greater simplicity and scantiness of dress a decade later, the stark absence of colour, or texture, or any status-conferring detail, all of which is captured with such clarity in the *Portrait of a Young Woman* (attributed to the circle of Jacques Louis David, *c*.1800) was the perfect foil to the shawl's picturesque qualities. The shawl is a fundamental accessory in defining neo-classicism in dress but its flattering decorative qualities also rendered it an indispensible compensation for the

The Marquise de Sorcy de Thélusson *(1790), by Jacques-Louis David. The Marquise is clearly in advance of French fashion, as this painting pre-dates the craze for shawls by eight or nine years.*
NEUE PINAKOTHEK ART MUSTUM, MUNICH

unflattering qualities of unadorned, unstructured
white shifts. Few women could renounce those
visual aids – colour, pattern, richness of texture –
on which they had long relied to enhance their
appearance. Dress at this period was in effect a
form of *undress*, a simulated nakedness. The shawl,
as the sole layer of substance, completed the
ensemble, allowing the wearer to feel dressed – or
at least, half dressed, which to some was better
than none:

> now all are reducible to two heads, viz. the
> undress and the half-dress – our belles are but
> half-dressed. Thus very few of them can plead
> the privilege of the *femme couverte*, save only
> and only except when the Cashmere shawl is
> thrown over their shoulders, leaving all
> uncovered and unprotected below it. (*Dress and
> Address*, anon., 1819, pp 50–1)

Within this combination of opacity and
transparency lies the paradox, however, that whilst
the shawl offered a veneer of modesty, its density
heightened the contrasting flimsiness of the muslin
dress.

Despite its eastern origins, the standard for the
draping of a shawl derived from classical art, and
thus a shawl worn 'gracefully' meant in imitation of
classical drapery with the additional ingredient of
the 'picturesque', a term more usually applied to
landscape. Capturing the movement of such drapery
became a popular theme in contemporary drawing
and painting, such as Antoine Berjon's *Merveilleuse
aux Pommes* (*c*.1795–7). The fascination for the
way in which drapery both revealed and concealed
the form did not remain confined to the surfaces of
paintings. The revival of classical drama in the
French theatre led by the actor François-Joseph
Talma, and the popularity of Lady Hamilton's
'attitudes', requiring several Kashmir shawls as
props to the fluid sequence of poses inspired by
classical vase painting and sculpture, demonstrated
to the fashion-conscious public a very different
approach to dress and a new standard of elegance.

Explicit reference to the classical mode became
a critical measure of the gentility of the wearer that

Merveilleuse aux Pommes
(*c.1795–7*), *by Antoine
Berjon*.
MUSÉE DES BEAUX ARTS, LYON

continued, despite various modifications,
throughout the 19th century, and in particular in
the admiration expressed for the skilful
manipulation of cloth into elegant folds. Thus the
exoticism of the Indian shawl became contained by
the discipline of classicism which still influenced
codes of dress as late as 1838, when an acerbic
entry in *The Young Lady's Friend* judged that: 'the
shawl is the same in value, whether it is dragged
round the shoulders like an Indian's blanket, or
worn in graceful folds' (vol. II, p 75). One can infer

that the ideal arrangement of the shawl, 'in graceful folds', expressed an aesthetic sensibility and cultural refinement that was notably absent in the 'native' manner of wearing it 'dragged round the shoulders'. Indeed, the shawl was not merely 'worn', it was tastefully displayed. The quality of the shawl alone would not automatically attract admiration and confer status; but the manner in which it was worn was the ultimate distinction between a lady of quality and her inferior imitator.

It was a great advantage to be tall and slender, not only at the peak of neo-classicism when the attenuated form was the most admired, but even in the mid-19th century. In Mrs Gaskell's *North and South*, published in 1855, Margaret's 'tall, finely made figure . . . set off the long beautiful folds of the gorgeous shawls that would have half-smothered Edith' (p 39). It was Margaret's height which enabled her to carry off the large Indian shawl 'as an empress wears her drapery' (p 99).

Precisely because it was a most important emblem of luxury the shawl established close links with nuptial preparations. Wealthy grooms established the custom of presenting the bride with a fine shawl as a wedding gift, which would then be worn as part of the wedding outfit. In 1800, Laure Permon, the future Duchesse d'Abrantès, was one of the first brides to receive several shawls amongst the wedding gifts presented to her by her fiancé, General Junot. Napoleon Bonaparte followed suit when he presented seventeen French cashmere shawls to his second wife, Marie Louise of Austria, at their marriage in 1810. Such generous tokens of affection established a close association between the shawl and romance: ' . . . women would resort to the refrain that a cashmere shawl was the only acceptable proof of true love' (*Journal des Dames et des Modes*, 1815).

By the second decade of the 19th century wearing a shawl as part of the wedding outfit was not unusual in England, either, even at modest weddings such as that attended by Jane Austen in 1814. The bride of her acquaintance wore 'a dress of fine white muslin, and over it a soft silk shawl, shot with primrose, with embossed white satin

flowers' (Penelope Byrde, *A Frivolous Distinction*, n.d., pp 22–3).

As the shawl became more readily available, so it came to form an important part of the middle-class bride's trousseau. In *North and South* the preparations leading up to the wedding of Edith Shaw are focused on the shawl: 'I have spared no expense in her trousseau . . . she has all the beautiful Indian shawls and scarfs the General gave to me, but which I shall never wear again,' boasts Mrs Shaw, the bride's mother (p 37). Despite the considerable competition from the French, English and Scottish manufacturers, the Indian shawl still enjoyed immense prestige and the reputation for luxury which could command a high price. Hence the lament of Mrs Shaw's friend, Mrs Gibson, whose recently married daughter 'had set her heart upon an Indian shawl, but when I found what an extravagant price was asked, I was obliged to refuse her. She will be quite envious when she hears of Edith having Indian shawls. What kind are they? Delhi? with the lovely little borders?' (pp 38–9).

As a ceremonial gift the shawl became associated with marriage and baptism, the rituals signifying the bonds of affection that linked bride to groom or parent to child. Even the bond of friendship might be marked by such an exchange, as illustrated by Amelia Sedley's generous donation of her white cashmere shawl to the less fortunate Becky Sharp in *Vanity Fair*. It became customary for a mother either to pass her own trousseau shawls on to her daughter when she got married, or to purchase new ones, as the above passages illustrate.

The acquisition of a shawl signalled an ascent of the social ladder. In Balzac's *La Cousine Bette* (1846) the eponymous character of the story becomes entranced by a particular shawl, a family shawl. Soon after her arrival in Paris she becomes consumed by the idea of possessing:

> that yellow cashemire given by the baron to his wife, in 1808, and that, according to custom in some families, had passed from the mother to the daughter in 1830.

For ten years the shawl had been well worn; but this precious fabric, always kept packed tightly into a sandalwood box, seemed, like the furniture of the baron, always brand new . . . (p 67)

After the wedding, the shawls would be carefully stored in a purpose-made chest, such as that used by Edmund de Goncourt's grandmother: '. . . made in the beautiful wavy, satiny sandalwood so sought after during the last century. This was where my elegant grandmother kept only the most beautiful of her cashmeres – she had so many of them' (*La Maison d'un Artiste*, Paris, 1880).

Not only the wearing but the storing of these luxurious and coveted items became a major focus in the ritual of femininity. They were traditionally scented with sandalwood or cedarwood, which were both moth preventatives.

So although the shawl became increasingly affordable and no longer representative of elite fashion – a development well illustrated by its ban from French Court dress in 1815 after Napoleon's exile (perhaps because of its strong associations with the court of the First Empire) – it continued to be worn with great pride. Jane Carlyle commented in a letter dated 1830 that: 'I am very vain of the beautiful little shawl; so vain that I rode to Templand with it above my habit'; from which one can conclude that the combination of habit and shawl was somewhat irregular.

Mrs Gaskell admirably captures the physical and psychological pleasure of wearing the shawl, at the moment where Margaret, modelling her aunt's shawls:

> . . . caught a glimpse of herself in the mirror over the chimney-piece, and smiled at her own appearance there – the familiar features in the unusual garb of a princess. She touched the shawls gently as they hung around her, and took pleasure in their soft feel and their brilliant colours, and rather liked to be dressed in such splendour. (*North and South*, p 39)

The market for shawls had become most profitable and put the fashionable shawl in reach of all middle-class women by the 1820s. Prices had dropped dramatically – a good quality cashmere cost around 100 guineas in 1800; a few years later the Empress Joséphine was spending between 8,000 and 12,000 francs but by 1814 a Paisley imitation could be had for a mere £12. By the date of the publication of *North and South* the European shawl trade had reached its peak in productivity, both in England and in France, and by 1860 the average price of a large Paisley shawl was 27 shillings. None the less, the Indian shawl held its own against such competition – a factor that retailers, such as The Great Shawl and Cloak Emporium in Regent Street (formerly the shawl warehouse of J & J Holmes) endorsed in their advertisements listing 'the largest and most magnificent collection in England . . . the latest designs of India, Gold, Delhi, Benares, Decca and Lahore' (A Adburgham, *Shops and Shopping*, London, 1989, p 99).

Genuine cashmere and French cashmere shawls continued to be extremely expensive but the woman who had to compromise on price could now select a reasonably priced shawl from the retail outlets in London, especially J & J Holmes who offered a comprehensive range of all types and all prices, from 1 guinea to 100 guineas, and yet could boast of a Royal Appointment. Another retailer in Regent Street, T Williams, offered a cleaning service and a second-hand department where customers could exchange their shawl for another.

It could be said that the acquisition of a shawl was easier, by the mid-century, than the wearing of it in the manner required – gracefully. As the silhouette in feminine dress expanded in its dimensions and accrued complex surface decoration, the shawl was obliged to accommodate itself to a quite different surface to that of the columnar muslin shift worn at the beginning of the century. It competed with other intense colours and the light-reflecting textures of silks rather than matt, plain muslin. The shawl rarely had direct contact with the skin (unless it was worn with evening dress, and even then such contact would have been limited), nor did it interact with the contours of the body. It shrouded rather than

Les Deux Soeurs (1843) by Théodore Chassériau. This double portrait shows very clearly how shawls were actually worn. These are both long shawls, or scarfs as they were sometimes called, and appear to be worn not so much for effect but for warmth. With the exception of the ends, the shawls are plain, a style that dates back to the early part of the 19th century (note that the shawl worn by Mrs John Crome in Plate 1 (1813–14) is very similar). The two shawls are probably family heirlooms.

MUSÉE DU LOUVRE/ RÉUNION DES MUSÉES NATIONAUX, PARIS

uniform manner in wearing the shawl. Women's magazines advised their readers to control the shawl by pinning their arms against their breasts. The effect was one of primness and stiffness which fettered movement. Like the bonnet, which limited the wearer's view and hearing of the world, the shawl was highly impractical and limited physical interaction with the world. Both were major contributors to the material expression of the feminine virtues of helplessness and dependency. But above all, for the middle class, the shawl denoted decorum and respectability.

Despite these changes the shawl was such a familiar accessory, in England and France, that it ranked as an extraordinarily powerful emblem of femininity – woman as ideal mother, woman as the alluring *femme fatale*. Flaubert, who had witnessed and admired the shawl as a accessory to erotic dance on his Egyptian travels, exploited the potentially fetishistic qualities of the shawl in his novel *Éducation Sentimentale* (1869). At the first meeting of the two lovers, it is her shawl that provides the young law student with an opportunity for gallant display, as he rescues it from trailing in the water: it thus brings them together for the first time, sparking the attraction between them. The image of the shawl nestling against her bare skin haunts the young lawyer, fuelling his mounting obsession: 'How many times, out at sea, on damp evenings, she must have wrapped it round her body, covered her feet with it, or slept on it!' (p 19).

In situations such as this in real life, the shawl could facilitate a form of intimacy and thus the careful attentions directed towards the shawl, that most cherished possession, became incorporated into the ritual of courtship. A true gentleman would always offer to carry a lady's shawl, taking it into his safekeeping, for such was its value: 'he [Dobbin] carried about Amelia's white cashmere shawl', even though 'the people laughed at seeing the gawky young officer carrying this female burthen' (Thackeray, *Vanity Fair*, 1847, p 90). The response of the onlookers to 'this female burthen' reveals just how strongly the shawl had become gendered in European society, despite its origins, in its native

defined the form. In addition, the shawl now had to compete with other accessories of equal importance. In short, it no longer held centre stage.

The disappearance of complex variations in draping was succeeded by a more simple and

India, as a male item of dress that was first adopted by European men living out there.

The shawl appears to have encapsulated all that was most admired in idealised femininity. In both visual and literary contexts the shawl is frequently used to signify the female body. In the same scene of *Vanity Fair*, Dobbin, with Amelia's shawl draped over his arm, admires her as she strolls with his rival companion: ' . . . he watched her artless happiness with a sort of fatherly pleasure. Perhaps he felt that he would have liked something on his own arm beside a shawl' (p 90).

The shawl may have offered an element of practicality in its warmth but clearly this was still the least that the aspiring woman sought from it. Its status as a fashion symbol for those who would have had little opportunity to dress fashionably is well illustrated in Mrs Gaskell's *Cranford* (1853) when an unsophisticated local is thwarted in his purchase of a 30-shilling shawl for his wife and sadly concludes that 'Lizzie must do on with her cloak for a while' (p 175). The inference is that the shawl was coveted because it was fashionable, while the cloak was merely functional.

However, the shawl did not disappear from the middle-class wardrobe because it was now affordable by the poor. It continued to exist at all social levels until the 1880s when it was transformed into tailored mantles. The point has already been made that the shawl could carry contradictory meanings and this applied to class associations as much as to moral or aesthetic ones. Thus the shawl could operate both as a symbol of the wealthy fashionable woman and as a symbol of destitution, according to its particular qualities, including condition, and the manner in which it was worn. This is well illustrated in the painting of *The Painter's Studio* by Gustave Courbet (1855) where the fashionable Madame Sabatier is shown wearing a beautifully embroidered silk shawl that contrasts with the tatty, soiled relic of a plaid shawl worn by the Irish woman nursing her child in the left foreground. The shawl is the means by which their relative position in society – that of affluence and destitution – is conveyed.

Sweethearts and Wives (1860) by John J Lee. The woman (probably a wife) has put on her best clothes, including a good-quality shawl. She expects to have to wait a long while, watching the ship make sail and leave. Possibly her husband is a petty officer and can afford to buy her a good shawl as a leaving present.
BY KIND PERMISSION OF ROY MILES GALLERY, BRUTON STREET, LONDON W1

As the shawl became more firmly established, in the second half of the 19th century, within the limited range of working-class fashion, it began to acquire negative associations that contrasted with its image of respectability and its endorsement of a definition of femininity that defined woman as frail, impressionable, pampered creatures in need of cosseting. In literature and painting the shawl began to be associated with the fallen woman or the dispossessed. Its expressive qualities could convey a state of dejection as readily as it had conveyed that of social superiority in earlier works. Precisely because the soft, brightly coloured shawl had a long reign as an emblem of dignified indulgence, it could carry a poignantly contrasting meaning when it was soiled and tattered. Its range of gestural meanings could instantly project an image of pathos, engaging the reader's sympathies. Thus in *David Copperfield*, when Dickens describes a young girl, her reputation sullied, as she stood 'absorbed in gazing at the water, . . . her shawl was off her shoulders, and . . . she was muffling her hands in it, in an unsettled bewildered way' (p 556), the reference to the disarray in her shawl movingly conveys her desperate state of mind as she contemplates suicide by throwing herself into the river.

Similarly, in Flora Thompson's autobiography and account of poor rural life in the 1870s, the shawl operated in complete reverse to its former image as an enviable and fashionable accessory. Again, it is the shawl which creates a heightened sense of pathos and measures the degree of deprivation to which its humble wearer is subjected. Bess continues to wear her Paisley shawl throughout her fifteen-year-and-more long courtship until 'At last came their funny little wedding, with Bess still in the Paisley shawl, and only her father and mother to follow them on foot through the allotments and over the stile to church' (*Lark Rise to Candleford*, 1939, p 1800).

By the 1860s the shawl was no longer an exclusive emblem of urban fashion but was widely worn and incorporated into rural wedding attire, in both France and Britain. This nuptial custom was extended, in France, to the baptism of the first-born child who was carried within the same shawl that its mother had worn for her wedding. Similarly, in Scotland, the 'kirking' shawl was worn on the first Sunday after the wedding and again after the birth of the first child. By the time of Flora Thompson's autobiography the shawl had become emblematic of working-class pride; no matter if it was threadbare, it retained its dignity and thus was worn for special, ritualistic, occasions only.

It can only be concluded that it took a number of complex developments in taste, commerce and manufacturing technology to pave the way for the shawl's considerable economic success and social prominence in the 19th century. Economic theory, however, does not suffice to explain the extraordinary resonant meaning that the shawl could convey both in real life and in its representations. It encapsulated a romanticised definition of the ideal woman appreciated by men and women alike. It was a key element in the culturally constructed mystique of femininity. Its chemistry of luxury and femininity constituted a powerful alchemy that transfigured its wearer. It is no wonder that the shawl was such an emotionally charged symbol and that its eclipse was mourned. As the garment fell from fashion, femininity lost its mystique:

> The importation of the shawl into France created a total revolution in women's dress and appearance. It was adopted, protected and put on a pedestal by fashion and quickly became the ultimate endorsement of elegance, the indispensible item of dress for anyone who prided herself on being well turned out . . . the feminine forms that the shawl allowed us to guess at while at the same time veiling them will now be put on view for our gaze; for the spectator could deduce what kind of woman he was dealing with just by the manner (it was one of the remarkable talents of the Parisienne) in which she was draped in a shawl, whether it was a tartan, a long Kashmir or a French one. Through subtle undulations, imperceptible movements of the shoulders, elusive curves, the trembling movement of the skin under the cloth that was in itself poetry, the upper class woman and the working class girl, seen from behind, wrapped in a shawl, could be distinguished instantly. The shawl was a decent and at the same time a graceful and majestic garment . . . let us mourn it, let us hope that its passing will be merely fleeting . . . (*Grand Dictionnaire*)

5 *The Shawl Designs and Fashion Today*

JUDY WENTWORTH

The origin of the Indian pattern found throughout the shawl industry has caused much conjecture. Its meaning and symbolism have given rise to much analysis and speculation, from serious academic and historical study to romantic supposition. One thing is as firm as a rock in all the seas of wishful thinking: the pine-cone, or *buta*, design has become an archetype which, whatever its origins, may be seen now in the decorative arts in most parts of the world.

Possibly due to its prevalence in the patterns on shawls worn by fashionable ladies of the 19th century, the pine-cone pattern seems today to be most suited to textiles. Perhaps its fluid shape adapts especially well to the movement of cloth when worn, draped or softly gathered; perhaps the underlying associations with tradition and luxury endow the motif with a subliminal familiarity. Most people will recognise the design, even if they cannot name it.

Many men will keep, among their ties, one or more printed with the pine-cone pattern. Some may own dressing-gowns or socks, or even more intimate wear, of wool, silk or cotton similarly decorated. The same appeal maintains the production of established styles of ladies' dress fabrics in silk, cotton and lightweight wools. But there is nothing static about the magical pine-cone.

Examples of the 20th-century use of the Indian pine-cone motif.
PHOTO: DAVID WICKS

33

A French-designed cashmere shawl with exaggerated pattern shapes of the 1860s. The illustration shows very clearly how a large shawl was folded and worn. From La Mode Illustrée, *9 June 1857.*

It can become whatever the designer's whim dictates.

The first twenty years of the 19th century produced both shawls with tiny sprigged grounds, sometimes with a central 'moon', and shawls with plain fields bearing end borders woven with a larger repeating pine-cone motif set on different coloured grounds, called 'harlequin' shawls. By the 1830s seaweedy and ferny fronds in pine shapes and background designs were fashionable, in both printed and woven shawls. There was a brief but spectacular vogue for exotic oriental and architectural decoration in the 1830s and 1840s, which produced woven masterpieces such as the 'Nou Rouz', 'Isphahan' and 'Denderah' shawls from France. This was superseded by the huge flower-filled pines of the vegetal style so prevalent in the late 1840s and early 1850s. These pines could be as long as 5 feet (1.5 metres) over a 12-foot (3.65-metre) shawl. Many such shawls were woven as show-pieces for the Great Exhibitions in London and Paris. Floral treatment of the swirling pine shape was especially notable in the high-quality shawls, both printed and woven, by the Norwich firm of Towler & Campin. By the 1860s the pine patterns of the superb all-silk shawls made by another Norwich manufacturer, Clabburn, Sons & Crisp, had moved into an almost Celtic phase, which may be seen as a precursor of the Art Nouveau movement. By this time the scope for change seemed infinite, but the fashion for shawls, no matter how innovative the designs, was dying.

To the modern textile designer it might seem that there are no avenues left to explore. This is not so. In Italy the textile industry is fortunate in having manufacturers not only sufficiently far-sighted and sufficiently passionate to have assembled important collections of antique shawls of every variety of the pine-cone pattern, but also practical enough to put these into use in their design studios and thence into commercial production. Their understanding and skilled use of colour, allied to current technical ability, has

permitted both woven and printed textiles to continue to develop the pine-cone's infinite variety of design and range of use.

The glittering world of *haute couture* selects dazzling versions of this old design and presents them in a fresh and exciting way. Whether embroidered, sequinned, appliquéd or printed, of cut velvet or lamé, whether bold and eye-catching or discreet and refined, hardly a year goes by in which the pine-cone motif is not seen on the cat-walks of the prestigious international fashion houses.

So too in interior design. Woven textiles, using subtle colours pleasing to the contemporary eye, are available for upholstery and furnishings. Some of these are so skilfully produced that, from a distance, they can deceive all but the most expert into believing that they are more than a hundred years old, bearing the gentle patina of age. Thrown over table or sofa, their ability to harmonise with mellow wood can enhance furniture and bring warmth and beauty to a room. Modern furnishing textiles are intended to be cut and shaped to meet the decorator's needs. It should be emphasised that fine antique pieces should never be converted into clothing, cushions or upholstery, as it is possible to lose valuable evidence for the textile historian. Too many masterpieces of the shawl weaver's craft have been so treated in the past, cut up to become sad remnants, and the unique information they bore has been thrown away and lost for ever. Fortunately public and private collections hold much information – and inspiration – for us all.

There is vast scope today for the textile designer and manufacturer with a sense of history. The commendable publication, in the past half-century, of serious studies of the shawl industry and of museum archives, eloquently indicates what riches may be unearthed. It is to be hoped, as the 20th century draws to a close, that the shawls held by the Norfolk Museums Service will bring as much delight to people today as they did to the leaders of fashion who wore them more than a century ago.

6 *Weaving Techniques*

RACHEL CHAPLE

This chapter reviews the development of early and pre-industrial weaving techniques in Europe, and how they influenced techniques used in the making of Norwich shawls.

Fabrics are made on looms which vary from the very simplest to heavy industrial machinery. Weaving in its basic form is, like darning, the interlacing of threads to form a web or cloth structure, the threads interlacing at right angles and at such a density as to create the required weight of cloth. This is also dependent on the type of yarn used and the fibre from which it is spun.

Taking darning as the simplest form of weaving, the hole in the fabric is firstly filled in with needle and thread in one direction and held under tension. This is in fact somewhat similar to a warp set up on a simple wooden frame. The cross threads are interwoven through the vertical threads with a needle alternately over and under to fill in the hole completely and make something approximating the original cloth in what is, in effect, the most used weave structure – plain weave or tabby. There are three basic actions in weaving: warp selection (making the shed), weft insertion (throwing the pick) and placing the weft (beating up). A loom is a machine which performs these functions and all looms which are powered by the co-ordination of the operator's hands and feet are handlooms. All the looms considered here are technically handlooms.

Typically, balanced plain weave, where the warp and the weft have equal weight and spacing and are often of the same yarn, is restricted to colour changes in either the warp or weft to make stripes or, with both together, to make checks. Twills,

which need three or more shafts, have a distinct diagonal line, and are also restricted in their design to stripes, diagonals, plaids and checks. Because the interlacings are fewer in number than in the same area of plain weave, the resulting cloth drapes well and has a more flexible and supple feel to it. European tapestry work, which is weft-faced, was, and is, used as a method of weaving pictorially, imitating paintings or similar designs. Only two shafts are needed. The warp is wound on to a frame or loom, firmly, making the basis of the cloth, while the design is woven with each colour of yarn wound onto individual bobbins, beaten down to cover completely the warp and built up to make the picture, pattern or design. This method is used by European tapestry weavers, American Indian rug and blanket weavers and Eastern kelim weavers, among others. The original Kashmir shawl used a combination of balanced 2/2 twill on four shafts for the ground cloth (over two and under two and the warp and weft showing to the same extent). The discreet patterns with their coloured yarn on small bobbins were hand-manipulated across the warp woven in a form of brocade similar in technique to European woven tapestry work. However, the ground warp and weft show throughout giving, characteristically, the twill diagonal to the pattern.

Ancient drawings show how early weavers started by stretching out measured warp threads and holding them under tension either on a frame; or by suspending weighted warps from an overhead cross bar (the warp-weighted loom); or by stretching the warp threads between two parallel bars the far one of which is tied to a fixed point and the near one attached to the weaver's body (backstrap loom). To keep the threads in the correct order, a stick would be put in the warp through alternate ends and pushed back giving a natural shed (opening) for the weft (the crossing thread). It was soon found that it was possible to tie loops on the other alternating warp ends to facilitate pulling the other ends up to form the other shed. These loops would either be left in small groups (for tapestry weaving) or tied onto another stick for plain weave.

The next development was the arranging of the two sets of loops as heddles on frames which were suspended so that they were then able to be operated by the feet from cords hanging from the harnesses which held the heddles. In many countries looms are still in use which have not developed much further than this. This may be partly because they are often used outside and the working parts complete with warp can be taken in at night if necessary. Also lightweight fabrics were made, and with light beating up of the cloth, strength in the frame of the loom was not important. By the time the shawls were coming into Europe weavers were using four or more shafts (sets of heddles on the harnesses) for more complicated fabric structures such as twills, satins, brocades and simple loom-controlled patterning. In Kashmir four shafts were used, on still very lightweight looms, to weave the twill ground for the shawls. Susi Dunsmore, studying weavers of eastern Nepal in 1980–1 with the Kosi Hill Area Rural Development Programme, found that though most of the weaving there is now in very fine cotton and on a plain-weave ground, they make beautiful repeat inlay patterns in a form similar to, though simpler than, the technique used in the 18th century in Kashmir. 'Raris', warm woollen blankets, are still woven in four-shaft twill with simple inlay in interlocking tapestry technique, the ground being white, the pattern in black and perhaps one extra colour only, but otherwise made in the same way as were the shawls.

In his reports to the India Office Moorcroft described the crowded workshops where these weavers worked. The floor looms, he says, were similar to those used in Europe, but inferior in workmanship, the factories containing up to three hundred of them. Two to three weavers worked at each loom. The pattern drawer made the design, conferred with the colourist and the scribe, after which the colourist pointed out the proportion of the colours, the scribe writing it out in a form of shorthand for the weavers to follow. Bobbins were prepared by winding on to each a short length of coloured yarn. The bobbins (a kind of eyeless needle) were made of smooth wood, with both their sharp ends slightly charred to prevent their becoming rough through use. Under the supervision of the colour master, the weavers next knotted the yarn from the bobbins in their proper places to the warp. They worked at the pattern on the loom from the back, with:

> the needles all hanging in a row, making from four to fifteen hundred according to the lightness or heaviness of the ornament. As soon as the designer is satisfied that the work in one line is completed the reed is brought down upon it, with a vigour and repetition apparently very disproportionate to the delicacy of the material. ('Notice of particulars respecting the manufacture of shawls in Kashmeer', 25 April 1821. MSS in India Office Library)

The original designs that were used in Kashmir were formal, ordered and with a regular spacing of the motifs. Although in a sense they were floral and semi-naturalistic they were unlike the figured brocade designs in fashion in Europe at the time. Their use of twill as the ground, instead of the more usual plain weave, gave a pronounced angular form to the motifs and designs which differed markedly from the European inlaid brocade or extra weft patterning.

Looms in Europe in the pre-industrial age were strongly constructed, often by the local carpenter or by the weaver himself, and were used mainly to weave worsted and the heavier woollen cloths for clothing and household use. Still comparatively simple, each loom would have had probably four shafts on balancing pulleys or jacks which were attached to treadles to that the weaver could easily operate the shed changes with his feet. The warp was stretched between the roller under the cloth beam at the front of the loom, over the breast beam, through the heddles to the back beam and wound round the warp beam. It was held under tension by the use of pawl and ratchet or by a releasing device and a weightbox for the warp roller.

The embellishment of fabrics whilst weaving, rather than by subsequent application of embroidery threads, goes back to the earliest days of weaving. On simple two-shaft looms, in order to pick up some of the warp threads for patterning in a predetermined order, several smooth sticks would be inserted in the warp as required for the pattern. But the sticks could only be used once, so the whole repeat would have to be picked out again. Even now, in parts of the Americas and Asia, smooth pattern sticks are laid in, removed and replaced, the sequence then repeated as required. With the introduction of the horizontal loom as opposed to the early upright frames, controlled pattern weaving became more widespread, and the methods more inventive. Many traditional peasant or folk designs were, and still are, woven in Europe on four-shaft floor looms controlled by foot pedals or treadles but the available patterns, though many, are limited. These patterns relied on variations of the way the warp was threaded through the heddles on the four shafts. Normally weaving would be done using two or four shafts, as most household and clothing textiles can be produced in this way and most manufactured woollen cloth would have used simple weaves relying on the colour, fulling and finishing for appeal.

Using looms with two or more shafts for the ground cloth, the next development was for the extra patterning sticks to be replaced by loops tied to sticks (pattern heddle rods) so that the selected warp threads could be lifted in order as before but remain in position permanently for that warp. Eventually, through other developments such as the cross-harness loom used in Persia, pattern heddle rods evolved into extra pattern shafts raised by drawstrings. The number of shafts used is limited by the fact that the weaver has to operate the changes with his feet, and few handlooms have as many as twelve shafts or more. Damask looms built and used in Sweden had extra shafts operated by individual cords ranged along the loom above the weaver's head and one was built over 100 years ago with one hundred shafts. There is a photograph in John Becker's *Pattern and Loom* (1987) of the loom being used by the original owner's daughter and it must be a very slow process as she seems to be having to refer to the design chart and count out the shafts to select before each throw of the shuttle. A similar so-called 'button loom' with the cords taken out to the side was used elsewhere in Europe for a time. The cords were pulled down using wooden knobs below in a horizontal frame, presumably by an assistant.

With the arrival of silk from the East, and the growing appreciation of and demand for luxury, came the drawloom, probably arriving via the Silk Road from China where a form of drawloom was known in or about the 6th century. Wherever silk was used much energy and inventiveness seems to have been applied to finding ways of making the most of its properties, and to raising and maintaining the standards of the textiles produced. Indian and Persian silk-weaving centres used, and still use, the cross-harness loom – a form of the drawloom. By the 9th century there was silk weaving round the Aegean and the Moors had introduced it to Spain and by the 12th century it was flourishing in northern Italy. Louis XI introduced Italian silk weavers from Milan to Lyons and Tours in 1480 and the use of the drawloom spread from there. Protestants driven from the Netherlands and France brought silk weaving to Kent, London and East Anglia in the late 16th century and with them came the drawloom. It brought with it the possibility of patterning with complex figuring, already popular for printed textiles, the designs of which were by this time floral, delicate, informal and graceful.

The handwoven tapestry-twill technique is very labour-intensive, a Kashmir shawl taking eighteen months to three years to complete. This could not have been considered in the developing industrial age in Europe and the drawloom was an ideal tool to adapt the technique. The silk warp would be put on in 'straight' threading for 2/2 twill in the main shafts of the loom, with the pattern warps also threaded through the mails of the drawloom.

The difference between a drawloom and a normal floor loom is that, built upon the existing framework of the floor loom and suspended behind the four or more shafts controlled by the weaver's feet, is the monture or mounting. This consists of extra heddles with glass or metal mails (eyes) individually weighted by a lingo (a wire weight of about an ounce) from which cords are taken up, gathered through the neck and taken above the loom. Early looms used a horizontal framework above the warp through which the drawcords were taken to keep them in proper order. This developed

into the comber board, a board with holes which not only fulfilled that function but also controlled the sett of the cloth. It could also then be used either to tie the cords to form repeat patterns across the warp or for point-repeat patterns, that is, where the pattern turns on itself giving a mirror image either at the centre of the piece or of the individual patterns. The 'point' is the warp end or weft pick at which the reversal begins and ends and was made use of in designs using the drawloom.

The illustrations of looms in ancient China and in the Near East today have the drawboy perched above the loom, but by the time the drawloom was used in Europe it was found advantageous to take the cords to the pulley box, set at about 45 degrees, over the pulleys and across horizontally (tail cords) to a nearby wall or firm fixing point and made fast. From these tail cords, simples (also cords), were

Engraving showing an early 18th-century drawloom with the drawboy at work. The weaver would sit on the bench on the left-hand side. Later versions allowed the drawboy to work on the floor level, with a drawfork to help him pull the heavy rows of simples. From Diderot's Receuil des planches sur les sciences, les arts libéraux et les arts méchaniques, avec leur explication, Paris, 1763.

tied and fixed vertically to the floor alongside one, or two, strong cords, known as guides, stretching from floor to ceiling. Then, working from the design, drawn out in detail and in colour on squared point paper (a special graph paper used by weavers), loops of string (the leashes) were tied for each line of pattern which were then fastened in correct order to the guides. The drawboy, selecting each pattern lift, could now, from floor level, pull down on the weight of the warp, rather that raising it. He then held it while the weaver threw the shuttle and beat up. Even pulling the leashes down must have been very heavy work, especially with a complicated design, because each pattern warp end to be raised weighed at least an ounce, but the drawboy was eventually helped by the invention of the drawboy's fork, or drawfork. Primitive forks to hold the drawcords between lifts had been used on earlier eastern looms but in Europe, because the drawboy worked from floor level, he was able to use the fairly elaborate mechanism which had been invented – the drawboy's fork. In effect, these were two strong prongs on a sliding attachment with a lever, mounted on a firm solid stand at the side of the loom near the guide cords. When a pattern row was required the drawboy carefully slid the higher prong under the next group of simples already picked out by the leashes and, pulling the lever forward, brought the lower prong into use as a fulcrum while raising the pattern warp ends with the upper prong. He thus needed to exert less effort. Sliding the attachment back, he would then select the next pattern lift and repeat the process.

The drawloom with the drawfork was very efficient and could produce quite complicated patterns. The disadvantages were that each new design took two weeks or longer to set up, especially as patterns became more and more complex, and it was easy enough for the drawboy to make mistakes, thereby devaluing the piece. By the 18th century drawlooms had become sophisticated, comparatively easy to use and still within the scope of the weaver himself to maintain. When firms began controlling their own designing, the patterns, both for the shawls and for the damasks and figuring used in the Norwich 'stuffs', would be worked out on paper before being transferred to the weaver to set up on his loom.

To develop the speed and accuracy of pattern weaving, many were working on improvements to the loom. In Italy weavers worked in commercial workshops and tended to be secretive about their proceedings, but in France, where the manufactories were State subsidised, knowledge was shared and several were working on automating the shed selection device. Among them was Basil Bouchon who, in 1725, worked with a roll of punched paper to help select the simples. Then, in 1728, a French mechanic, Falcon, invented a chain of cards revolving round a square cylinder. Both these were operated by the drawboy using a treadle, but in 1745 Jacques de Vaucanson placed the cards and cylinder back above the loom and the drawcords and used blades or griffes, again operated by a treadle, to raise the drawcords. Joseph Marie Jacquard combined these ideas using de Vaucanson's griffes as the lifting device and Falcon's chain of pattern cards, this machine being patented under Jacquard's name in 1801 and 1804. It met with much initial resistance from the workers, as it was seen as competition to their labour. The machines were expensive, their productivity was comparatively low and they were only really suited to complex weaves where they had great advantages over the drawloom. The Jacquard was the first automated selection mechanism and, after several improvements, by mid-century was in use throughout Britain, including Norwich. There is evidence that attempts were made in Norwich to produce mechanical labour-saving devices because as early as 1687, Joseph Mason, a Norwich weaver, was granted a 14-year patent for an 'engine' for use with the drawloom which dispensed with the drawboy but, although other weavers seem to have used it, the patent was not renewed.

An important invention of the mid-18th century was John Kay's fly shuttle. Instead of throwing the shuttle by hand it was propelled by a jerk of the picking stick along the shuttle race and into one of the boxes at either end. Instead of using alternate

The pattern cards on a Jacquard loom in the Bridewell Museum, Norwich.

hands to throw the shuttle, this was now done by one hand which freed the other to work the batten and beat up the cloth. Not only did this double the speed of weaving but when his son Robert Kay invented the drop box thirty years later it was possible to use a variety of shuttles, introducing different colours consecutively in the weft. The drop box usually consisted of two or four shuttle boxes aligned above each other on either side of the batten and shuttle race. These could be raised or lowered by the weaver as he beat up. The model of a drawloom displayed in the Paisley Museum has ten boxes either side – a 'ten lay box' – enabling ten shuttles with different colours to be used as required.

The beautiful, lightweight shawls that were brought back from Kashmir were silky, lustrous,

warm and very desirable, and soon became a fashionable item to wear over the dress of the day. The state of development of textile machinery at this time is important because it influences how the shawls were woven by British and French manufacturers in their attempts to emulate the Kashmir originals. The weaving technique they set out to copy was the tapestry-twill with its ornamentation and soft drape and a search was set up to find a suitable yarn. The original cashmere fibre, the soft undercoat of the Tibetan goat's belly, was, of course, found to be scarce and expensive.

Attempts were made to procure Tibetan goats and farm them in Britain but without success. Spinners experimented on behalf of the weavers of Edinburgh and Norwich to recreate the qualities of cashmere. As the thread used for the warp had to be strong and elastic in order to take the extra tension produced when the shed is changed, most shawls were eventually woven with a silk warp, with silk or wool for the ground weft, but wool was always used for the fillover weft.

Edinburgh weavers may have been the first to attempt to copy the style and effect of the handwoven Kashmir shawls as there is mention of brocaded shawls being woven in 1792. But in Norwich the shawl trade was developing and at first, in the 1790s, the designs were printed onto the fabric and closely darned. This, from a little distance, gave the illusion of patterned weaving. By the beginning of the 19th century, the cloth was woven, in twill, face down, the weaver seeing only the reverse. The pattern would be concealed by the floats or 'fillovers'. These were formed because the extra weft threads were only required in parts of the patterns and when the shuttle was thrown from selvedge to selvedge. The weaver would not be able to see any fault arising so he was dependent on his drawboy pulling the cords in the right order. The floats make the basic difference between the European copies and the original Kashmir weaving where, with hand-manipulated applied tapestry weaving, the weft ends were returned within the motif. Because these floats added to the weight of the shawl, part of the finishing process was their trimming and removal by cropping, that is, they were trimmed back almost to the fabric itself, leaving an attractively coloured velvety surface on the reverse. In one shed the pattern could call for several throws of different colours through separate pattern lifts but the wefts were firmly beaten in by a following ground weft in the twill sequence so that, although the cropped ends could be quite short, they were safely held.

In *The Paisley Shawl and the Men Who Produced It* (1904), Matthew Blair, a Paisley native (who had known and been instructed by the 'grand old Paisley weavers', and the best years for weavers in Paisley had been the early years of the shawl trade) describes the weavers' life in 1879:

> In those times, weavers were to some degree their own designers – they worked out their ideas on their looms. They worked out ways to adapt their looms to accomplish new fabrics. Vast mechanical skill was exercised by these weavers in a series of inventions now forgotten. They were workmen who for general intelligence have no counterpart today. The occupation of weaving was favourable to intellectual development. Later a division of labour and the use of mechanical appliances kept the weaver from exercising these abilities. With the Jacquard attachment, a new type of workman appeared; the old cultured and ingenious weaver gradually disappeared.

The same could be said of the early Norwich shawl weavers.

The 19th century was in general a period of experiment and development. At the start of the century weavers were working in their homes or in small workshops and on looms which they were able to maintain themselves. The drawloom was a comparatively simple mechanical adaption of their own looms, but to buy the Jacquard machine was beyond the means of most. This meant that weavers started to work in manufactories as employees, the looms were maintained by specialist mechanics and trained designers worked on the ever-more elaborate motifs. Yet weaving was still a craft-based, rather than an industry-based occupation. The most important change for the weaver was that with the Jacquard machine, the leashes, simples and drawboy were replaced by a mechanism driven by a single foot treadle controlled by the weaver himself while the designer, no longer constrained by the drawloom, could make use of the flexibility of the machine which, with its use of punch cards, was able to control or raise every single warp end individually if required so that very complex or ornate designs could be woven. It was a time of innovation and industrial change. Designs generally became very elaborate and more mechanical looking, but this change was gradual and coincided with the growing European fascination with machinery and its products. High technical standards were accepted and sought and producers of the later shawls were artists and engineers overcoming technical problems and exploiting the structure of the weave.

The continuous chain of linked strips of firm card used Falcon's idea of a squared cylinder. Each equal-sized card is punched with the relevant number of small holes corresponding in position and number to the warp ends in that shed which have to be lifted following the pattern design and then linked in a continuous chain. By depressing the treadle the four-sided cylinder was made to revolve once, thus carrying round the next card to be presented in its turn. At each of these turns the griffe lifted one pick for a throw of the shuttle. Perforations in the cards let the spring either hold or let go of (therefore raise or not raise) the individual warp thread. The punching of the cards, a skilled operation, was done with the help of a machine which followed the designer's pattern. Each separate colour weft needed a separate card. Even during the weaving of a piece the designs could quite easily be changed. This was done by removing or inserting cards in the pattern chain, and, when the run of shawls was completed, the cards could be removed and stored, and perhaps used again later with cheaper yarns for the cheaper market.

As the weaving of the patterns became more elaborate and structurally sophisticated there was a movement towards a form of double-faced cloth which would make the shawls reversible.

It is recorded that in the 1840s a Paisley manufacturer, John Cunningham, developed a shawl woven with both sides patterned. A little later we have, in Norwich, the following account of 1854 describing the Persian Silk Ling Shawl invented by Messrs Clabburn, Sons & Crisp:

> By a combination of colours in the warp and only a small number of shoots, they have succeeded in producing that which, in all the fillover shawls, was produced by a number of different coloured threads, thrown in by an equivalent number of shuttles, and which, being arranged according to the design, formed one shoot. In the fillover shawl, the superfluity of material on the underside of the manufacture remained and was obliged to be cut off, causing a great waste of material, and, of course, increasing unavoidably both the labour and amount of cost.
>
> In the Persian Silk Shawl the warp is used to form part of the figure, in some instances, with a variety of colours, in others, with a single colour; the number of shuttles is thus reduced, and waste of material (nearly $\frac{2}{3}$) avoided.
>
> The shoot also is firmly bound in the process of weaving, thus lightness and strength are combined. The Jacquard loom principle is very ingeniously adapted to the old fillover loom in forming the pattern and thus the tire-boy [drawboy] has been rendered unnecessary. (*Norwich Mercury*, 5 May 1854)

Double cloth can take several forms. The one best known to handweavers is plain double cloth in which two warps, often of different colours, are woven simultaneously on the loom, the warps and wefts interchanging to form a simple pattern. Welsh double cloth, made up into coats or used as blankets, is a well-known example of this and although each fabric layer is separate from the other, they interchange often enough to keep the fabric firm and stable. The method used by Clabburn, Sons & Crisp for the Persian Ling Shawl is a form of double cloth, again using two warps one over the other and weaving them simultaneously. But in this case the weft is very carefully planned to interlace the two warps continuously across from selvedge to selvedge so that the different colours used are brought out in the patterns that are being made, on both faces. The Jacquard made this approach possible. These reversible shawls, an achievement in themselves, are far removed from the original Kashmir shawls. The designs, flowing freely, no longer display the twill ground which gave the early shawls a resemblance to the authentic Kashmir work.

There was a demand from the public not only for cheaper but also for lightweight versions of the shawl and this led to printing the designs onto specially woven fabrics. The cheap versions were printed, sometimes with lack of care, onto any suitable fabric, but for the fashionable to wear in summer, silk was used to produce a sheer, translucent, loosely woven fabric. Very loose plain weave is not stable in use so a fairly sophisticated form of weaving called gauze or leno was used. Leno, a form of plain weave, makes use of a twisted warp technique for controlling the structure of the fabric. The crossing warp ends are passed from side to side of the standard (fixed) ends and each crossing and recrossing of the warp must be held in place by the beaten-up weft or wefts. This is achieved by having half-heddles, called doups, only used for and unique to leno, on two extra shafts. These doups were of string until the invention of the flat steel doup heddle.

The methods used by the Norwich weavers, to reinforce what could be a fairly fragile fabric, varied. Some have ¾-inch self-coloured stripes of 3/1 twill in the warp crossed by similar stripes of plain weave in the weft. These stripes, in spite of the overprinting, are still prominent yet attractive in themselves. Others have only a 1-inch stripe of a more closely set warp in plain weave an inch in from each selvedge in warp and weft to reinforce the borders, while some, which have a slightly more closely set fine warp and weft, are plain and must have been considered as not needing the reinforcing stripes.

The technical achievements which have been outlined above are not specific to Norwich weavers or inventors, but they did make use of and benefit from them. Fine and intricate weaving had always been a part of Norwich industrial life since the 'Strangers' were encouraged to settle in the mid-16th century and this tradition was a determining factor in the early success of the Norwich shawl industry.

Built in 1839, this factory has had several different names. Originally known as the Norwich Yarn Company's Mill, or St James Factory, it is better known today as St James Mill, and houses the Jarrold printing and publishing firm. By Norwich standards it was a very large mill and was let off in floors to various manufacturers. It held 65 spinning frames and 500 power-looms. The lower engraving of Willet & Nephew in chapter 3 shows one of the floors in use.
BRIDEWELL MUSEUM, NORWICH

7 The Dyers and Printers of Norwich

HELEN M HOYTE

As the 19th century advanced, the dyers of Norwich earned a growing reputation for the excellence of their work. Newspapers and comments from the 18th century onwards provide glimpses of their achievements, with notable reference to the colour which was to become known as 'Norwich Red'.

It is perhaps surprising that the hard water of East Anglia suited the dyeing industry. Traditionally the city had been an important centre for madder dyeing; obtained from a plant grown locally, it dyes well in hard water. An old street in modern Norwich, St John Maddermarket – where the red vegetable dye extracted from the madder roots was bought and sold – recalls the thriving industry of the Middle Ages.

There were other natural advantages. Saffron was produced at Walsingham in north Norfolk; woad, indigo and alum were available and could also be imported from the Continent through Great Yarmouth, whence they were transported upriver to Norwich. And there was plenty of water, essential to the dyer. It is interesting to note that there seem to be no records of complaints from the citizens of Norwich, who presumably had their water supply polluted by noxious dyes, chemicals and metals used in the dyeing process in the heart of the city! Though some of the dye-houses were located upstream, many were situated in the heart of the city between Coslany Bridge in the west and White Friars Bridge, just north of the Bishop's Palace, and along to the lanes running down from King Street. Noxious dyes, chemicals, and metals which were used in the dyeing process were washed into the River Wensum.

From 1783 the numbers of dyers in the Norwich trade directories fluctuated. Some are listed as 'Scarlet Dyers' in recognition of their work being a separate branch of the trade. Others offer a cleaning service, like J Hannet who 'cleans and dyes . . . fill-over shawls, painted ditto, and lace veils cleaned and dressed like new . . . ' (*Norwich Mercury*, 27 April 1815).

The reference to 'painted' shawls appears again in 1820, and may indicate 'pencilling' or the practice of painting small areas with dye colours on shawls, after larger areas had been printed by blocks.

The following advertisement on the back of a letter outlines the service offered by dyers. After thanking his friends for their patronage, and announcing that his son has joined the partnership, Wm Yarington of De Caux's Court, St Simon and St Jude, Norwich, informs the public that his establishment will: 'Dye and Dress Silks, China Crapes, Zephyrs, Shawls, Cloths, Bombazines, Cottons, Moreens, Satins etc, and pledge themselves that every article with which they may have the honour to be entrusted shall be executed with neatness, punctuality and dispatch. Shawls of every description cleaned and dressed' (Castle Museum Archives, Norwich).

Access to a good water supply was essential to the dyers and bleachers who had established themselves beside the bridges and in small lanes running down to the River Wensum, in the north of the city. King Street, Elm Hill and Calvert Street remain today, but Blogg's and Cook's Yards, Little Cockey Lane and Luckett's Yard have long gone. Fields on the outskirts of the city were used as

Interior view of the dyehouse owned by Grout & Co. The style of dress dates the photo to c.1910–14, but the dyehouse and the working conditions endured by these men clearly had not changed since the mid- to late 19th century. The man on the far right, Bert Nichols, was the Assistant Dyehouse Manager. He died of tuberculosis in 1930.
BRIDEWELL MUSEUM, NORWICH

bleaching greens, traditionally used to whiten cloth.

Dyeing at that time could be described as an art rather than a science. The chemical explanation of how dyes worked and the effects that were achieved was only understood as the study of chemistry grew. Until an understanding was obtained of how fibres were penetrated and affected by dyes, and of the action of salts and metals, dyeing was very much a 'rule of thumb' craft.

Working conditions must have been arduous because of the nature of the processes. Constant quantities of hot and cold water were required, and dangerous acids (sulphuric and acetic), minerals (chrome, lead nitrate and copper) and salts (sodium chloride), caustic soda, urine and many other substances were involved. The preparation and processes employed are now inconceivable to the modern world.

There are no contemporary records of the dyeing industry in Norwich, but an account in Sharp's *London Magazine* of 6 March 1847 provides an impression of conditions in a dyeing factory at that time:

> The dye house is at least 150 feet long, under one roof, streams of liquid dye which discharge from the numerous vats are constantly pouring along and into the centre of the floor . . . woollen yarns scour in ammonia and soap . . . spun silks toss in boiling water. Loops of yarn hang dripping from dyers' pins and are dipt in vats and boilers. The vats are cast-iron, 6½ feet deep.

Before the introduction of rubber, leather must have offered some protection for the dyers, who worked in an atmosphere of wet heat for long hours, lifting heavy piles of dripping cloths constantly in and out of hot and cold water. Ammonia, chlorine, sulphuric acid and many other chemicals were a daily hazard. These conditions must have been common to Norwich and explain perhaps why so many public houses are listed in the trade directories!

Families guarded their colour recipes jealously, and a dyer's recipe book was his most prized possession. The notebooks would have recorded the quantities and mixtures of dyestuffs, the mordants used, the washing times and the number of dips by which the required colour developed. It was a well-known fact that two dyers using the same recipes and procedures could obtain different shades of the same colour. Strange practices arose which had no basis in chemistry, but because they had appeared to work by accident and had been successful were continued. K G Ponting, in his *Dictionary of Dyes and Dyeing* (1961, p 58) says that ' . . . a dead cat was thrown into the dye bath, whereupon things improved'!

The first mention of the colour later known as 'Norwich Red' appears in an obituary notice in the *Norwich Mercury*, 23 June 1759: 'Mr Ben Elder, who greatly improved the art of scarlet dyeing in this City'. The *Mercury* later reports the growing reputation of the dyers: 'By the middle of the 18th century the dyers of Norwich had become pre-eminently known for the beauty of their dyeing, so that worsted textures were forwarded from all parts of England to be dyed'.

One man who had a significant impact on the rising reputation of Norwich dyeing was Michael Stark. His obituary appears in the *Mercury* of 23 February 1831 and tribute is paid to his contribution to the wealth of the city:

> Died this day at his house at Thorpe, Mr Michael Stark aged 83. Mr Stark was a native of Scotland and descended from an ancient and honourable family in the County of Fife. He was apprenticed to a dyer and having been engaged in London was induced to come to Norwich. To Mr Stark, Norwich was indebted for the introduction of many valuable discoveries and improvements which tended considerably to the success of its manufactures.

There is no indication as to which dyer 'induced' Michael Stark to come to Norwich, but a scarlet dyer Thomas Aggs is listed in the 1783 Trade Directory, giving his address as 'Moon and Stars' Colegate Street. In the trade directory for 1811 Stark & Sons give their address as 'Moon & Stars, Colegate', which would indicate a link with Thomas Aggs. From 1830 onwards, according to the directories, Stark & Sons established their dyeworks in Duke Street.

Born in 1748, Michael Stark appears to have been a chemist of note, at a time when the mysteries of the art of dyeing involved chemical processes arrived at by accident and experiment. He corresponded with the foremost chemists of the day. His introduction of indigo and cudbear dyes, as well as chlorine gas to bleach cloth in the dye-house, resolved the uncertain practice of spreading cloth to air-bleach in the fields.

In association with Messrs Sime and Pitchford, Stark succeeded in producing a very fine scarlet which dyed both wool and silk yarns to the same colour. To be able to dye mixed fibres together was a valuable advance. Until then it had been almost impossible to dye mixed threads of silk, cotton, or silk and wool to a uniform shade of colour.

Mrs Barwell said of Stark in her foreword to

A Companion to the Norwich Polytechnic Exhibition (1840):

> Another source of prosperity for Norwich was the excellence of its dyeing. Mr Michael Stark devoted his life to improvements in the dyeing business; and the reputation the manufacturers of Norwich have borne for excellent colours is mainly owing to him and his sons. His eminence in one department, the dyeing and dressing of black bombazines brought nearly every piece in Kidderminster and Yorkshire to Norwich to be dyed. To the disgrace of human nature bribery and treachery were set on foot to obtain the secret and the villany of a confidential servant deprived Messrs Stark in a great measure of the advantages they must have enjoyed.

Mrs Barwell thus testifies to the fact that industrial espionage has always been with us!

Michael Stark had four sons. One, James (1794–1859), trained with John Crome and became a prominent member of the Norwich School of painters. An edition of the *Norwich Mercury* in 1831 described him as 'the son of a Scottish dyer, who is a man of considerable scientific and literary culture'.

An older son, William (1787–1863), was active in the family business and was described in his obituary as 'one of the most eminent chemists of his day, and particularly distinguished as one of the foremost dyers of fabrics in Norwich manufacture' (*Norwich Mercury*, 11 November 1863). As the industry declined, he gave evidence to the Commissioners on the plight of the textile workers in 1838, in which he was highly critical: 'The spirit of party politics is carried to such an extent here as to be totally destructive to the morals and intellectual acquirements of the working population' (*A Commission to Report on the Conditions of the Hand-loom Weavers*, 1839).

William Stark was the first signatory in a letter which the dyers of Norwich published in the *Norwich Mercury* on 23 December 1820, announcing that they would accept no further

goods for dyeing and dressing because of bad debts, unless their right to retain the goods in lieu of payment was recognised. Eighteen dyers signed – an indication of hard times.

It would seem that the best years of the Norwich textile trade were during Michael Stark's lifetime and owed much to him. Confirmation of the fame of Norwich Red might be taken perhaps from the arrangements made for the Norwich Crape Ball in 1826 at the Assembly House. It was organised to raise money to relieve the plight of unemployed weavers. All the ladies attending (apart from the patronesses) 'wore Scarlet Geranium coloured crape, trimmed according to their taste' (*Norwich Mercury*, 12 January 1826). The gentlemen were requested to wear waistcoats of shawl fabric.

By the middle of the 19th century the use of natural substances for dyestuffs declined. Plants, lichens and insects had been crushed and dissolved in chemicals since ancient times – often without full understanding as to how they worked – until the discoveries and developments of William Henry Perkin in about 1856, who, building on the work of Hofmann of Germany (whose student he had been), produced colours from coal-tar, and marked the first steps of a change to synthetic dyeing by manufacturers. The new dyes were much brighter than those obtained from natural substances and created new fashions in fabrics.

Sadly, the disastrous fire in August 1994 at Norwich Central Library, where the Norfolk Local History Library archives were stored, may have destroyed a substantial amount of information about the Norwich manufacturers. However, an 1867 dyer's notebook written in stylish copperplate handwriting and retained at the Bridewell Museum, Norwich, gives an insight into dyeing practices. Most alarming is the reference to tasting to test the dye: ' . . . add each time one glass of vitriol the acid taste should always prevail'! This unknown dyer, who worked at E & F Hinde, records the times for washings and boilings. Recipes are given for the weights of dyestuffs and mordants. Synthetic dyes are used alongside natural dyestuffs and include the range of reds he obtained from using safflower, sumac and magenta crystals.

The long association between Scotland and East Anglia through farming and fishing had cultivated a preference, within the textile industry, for the advantages that the Norwich textile manufacturer could offer. At the time when the best and most expensive shawls were made in Edinburgh, ' . . . the manufacturers sent their spun silk that required to be dyed scarlet and crimson to Norwich, and many hundreds of pounds weight annually were received from various Scotch houses' (*Norfolk Annals*).

J Telford Dunbar in his *History of Highland Dress* (London, 1962), quotes the complaint of one Scottish customer in 1800 that: 'The Norwich manufacturer adds only a penny for the same quantity of that colour (red) for which you charge 6d'. Stiff competition was offered, and for a long time Norwich was the main supplier of tartans to the Highland Regiments.

There must have been a wealth of information in the recipe books kept by the dyers but sadly the secret of the Norwich Red appears to have perished with them. Similarly, very little is known about the manufacturers of Norwich who printed shawls, apart from what may be gleaned from their advertisements.

There is a curious comment in the *Journal of Design and Manufactures* (1813) about a firm Higgins & Clarke, of Norwich, 'Various additions and improvements . . . by Higgins and Co, who brought the printed spun-silk shawl into notoriety'. Perhaps the simulation of the woven shawl by a printed copy gave offence to some. However, the light weight of the gossamer silk printed shawls must have found favour, for summer fashions.

The 1825 Book of Trades, reviewing calico printing, reports:

> Calico printing is reckoned a very good business for the master and his journeyman; the master however required a large capital and a ground for bleaching and drying cloths. He employs three sorts of hands; the pattern cutters of the types who are also the operators in printing, and a number of labourers to assist in washing. The pattern drawer is paid according to the variety and value of the designs; and the printer who is able to cut with ability and taste can, in the summer months, earn 4–5 gns a week or more. (p 83)

To print an image one block is required for each colour. Using six blocks appears to have been customary in the printing of Norwich shawls,

The printing surface of a wooden printing block is formed by hammering fine flattened brass or copper wires into grooves in the wood. This block was used for printing

Norwich shawls, although there is no shawl in the collection carrying this pattern.
BRIDEWELL MUSEUM, NORWICH

which comprised borders and centres. These were built up by placing the blocks to create a complete design over the square or oblong cloth. The skilful printer obtained different effects by varying the colours applied with the blocks. He could also change the design by printing a border with different fillings, and by leaving undyed areas he could alter the density of a design. *Trompe-l'oeil* became a challenge to designers and printers, and by the use of different mordants the colour of the dyes could be changed.

Wooden blocks had to be resistant to warping. Made up of two or three planks of wood pegged together, they could measure up to 3 inches thick and as much as 18 inches square, though a block weighing over 10 pounds was too heavy for the printer. Sycamore, beech, pear tree, holly and box wood were used.

A design was drawn onto the block in lamp black (carbon substance formed by the smoke of an oil lamp) and the part of the design to remain standing was marked out. The rest of the wood was cut away with sharp pointed knives and chisels. In the making of the block the repeats of the design motifs at each side of the block were skilfully integrated to fit neatly. Pin marks at the edges acted as a register and guided the printer as he placed the blocks. Wooden blocks were flocked to provide an absorbent surface for the dye. The shawl cloth was ironed onto the gummed surface of the printing table which had a resilient covering.

The front and back of a printing block. The blocks were built up in layers, to enable them to withstand repeated use. The smaller drawing shows the thumb and finger grip holes on the back of the block. For blocks weighing over 10 pounds a pulley was used, worked by the printer's foot and guided by his hands.
HELEN HOYTE

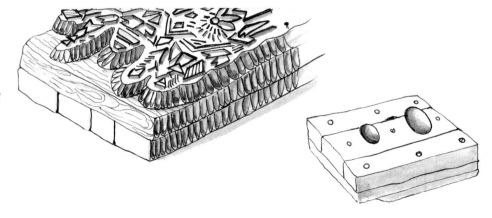

A mid-19th-century illustration showing textile workers printing by hand.

From The Illustrated Exhibitor and Magazine of Art, *vol. II, London, 1852, p 56.*

For some designs a 'lead' block was applied to the fabric first to give the fine lines of the pattern (these lines were often hatched to simulate the woven shawl) and was then followed by the colour printing blocks. Holes on the back of the block allowed the printer's thumb and fingers to grasp the wood.

Beside the printer stood a round shallow receptacle covered with a stretched leather upon which floated the dye in dissolved gum, and over that a thick blanket which acted as an ink-pad by feeding the block evenly with dye. A 'tearing' or 'tiering' girl or boy brushed the blanket to bring the dye to the blanket surface which provided an even surface of colour.

The printer placed the patterned side of the block on the dye blanket to charge it with colour, taking care that only the standing parts picked up the dye. It was then positioned on the cloth, and using a 'maul' or printers mallet he struck the block on the back to make a strong and even print.

The reverse of block-printed cloth shows rich colour and saturation of dye, and an even impression according to the pressure applied by the mallet. Bad block printing is blotchy and uneven on the back and the register of blocks and colours is faulty.

One colour had to dry before the next was applied. Working on wide tables, the printers built up complex patterns, having to fit the designs to the four corners of the shawl print, and creating the smooth progression of the elements of the design.

When printing was finished, the shawl might bear little resemblance to its intended colours. These developed in the fixing process when the cloth was steamed. After steaming, the cloth would have several washes in cold water followed by a hot wash in soap and several rinses to remove the last impurities. It was dried and the fabric's warp and weft were straightened.

Between 1844 and 1849 Clabburn & Plummer registered nine of their printed shawl designs at the Public Record Office. Towler & Campin also registered their block designs between 1846 and 1848. None of these designs are found in the collection, but two blocks made from these designs are kept at the Bridewell Museum, Norwich, and may have been cut by Joseph Nellor, whose name appears as a 'Block Cutter at Shickle & Towler' in the 1842 census.

The *Norwich Mercury* of 6 October 1836 reports a manufacturer changing from dyeing to printing:

> G Gedge most respectfully announces that in consequence of repeated solicitations both from London and Norwich houses that he would introduce the Printing Department into this City when he has completed the arrangements for this purpose which are now in full operation on Challis, Mousseline, de Laine, Parramattas, Bandannas, Shawls etc etc . . .
>
> NB: Dyeing, Dressing, Storing, Scouring on the usual terms, St Miles and St Swithins.

The craft of the cutter who made the wooden blocks for the printer was an exacting one. A few men give their occupation as 'Pattern Cutters' in the trade directories, but whether they were cutters of blocks is not clear.

The reference in the Book of Trades indicates that manufacturers employed their own in-house cutters, though freelance craftsmen were also employed. The complexity of the blocks can be seen at the Bridewell Museum, Norwich, which houses some superb examples of the block maker's craft. Unfortunately, only a few blocks remain – perhaps when firms went out of business, blocks made useful kindling, or succumbed to woodworm.

The making and cutting of blocks was expensive. A sudden change in fashion could mean a serious loss of investment and profit for a print works. An idea of the relative cost of the blocks can be seen below. In July 1795 the firm of 'R Bidwell and J Jarrold agreed to enter into partnership', and among the utensils of trade listed are:

Print board and tressels	–	15 shillings
Printing blocks	–	£9. 16s. 6d.
		(Jarrold family archives)

In the 1780s patterned shawls produced by the manufacturers Harvey & Knights were embroidered. An outline of the design was printed by block in water-colour onto the shawl material. The stitchers followed these guidelines to create the design. At the end of the 18th century simple flower patterns with borders and sprig motifs were fashionable. As block making developed, designs became more complex and by the middle of the 19th century the entire shawl could be covered with twisting pines, vines and geometric abstracts of flowers and leaves. It took great skill by the block maker to inset fine flattened copper wires in tiny pieces, and copper pin heads which created the many delicate lines and shadow effects of the printing surface.

In 1831 the excise duty on printed cloth was lifted and roller printing began to replace block printing, thus bringing prices down to within the reach of the working classes. Consumers of high-class, labour-intensive designs such as those required for shawls, continued to demand a high standard of craftsmanship which the exclusive block-printed shawls met. In their survey, the Commissioners examining the protection of patterns and designs remarked: 'Ladies of property will not buy a shawl of which there are many designs.' Exclusivity was vital to the lady whose maid was now appearing in printed fabrics!

In her researches into the firm of Charles Swaisland at Crayford in Kent, renowned for its excellence in block printing, Wendy Hefford, Deputy Curator of Textiles at the Victoria & Albert Museum, discovered that shawls had been sent from Norwich manufacturers to be printed at Crayford. The relative costs may be judged by an 1858 report in Sharpe's *London Magazine*: '1 to 10 gns for woven shawls, more for special ones. 2 gns for printed ones. It takes 1 week to weave a shawl, during which 20–30 printed ones can be produced.'

No records of the practices employed in the print works in Norwich in the early 19th century have survived, but other contemporary observers make it clear that as manufacturing changed from the cottages to the mills, working conditions in the early 19th century deteriorated. In the conditions in which they worked, it is indeed an achievement to have produced these delicate and intricate prints on gossamer silks and fine wools, which were worn as elegant shawls over so many years.

8 *The Weavers of Norwich*

PAMELA CLABBURN

Norwich had been a textile-producing city for so long that by 1785 there was no shortage of weavers who were ready and able to turn their hands to a new skill. In essence shawl weaving was little different from the weaving of 'stuffs'. These were often, though not always, made with a silk warp and wool weft as were many of the new-fangled shawls. In India the shawls which were to be copied in Europe were woven of wool, but in England no wool could be found capable of giving the required strength combined with softness to the fabric, so the compromise was to mix silk, or sometimes cotton, with fine wool. This the Norwich weavers were very competent to do.

It is not always easy to decide what is meant by the term 'weaver'. The word is used to describe the man who actually wove a piece of cloth, but it does not describe his status. In most cases he was a journeyman who had served his apprenticeship, which in weaving could start at the age of eleven or twelve, but could probably not find the capital or did not have the ambition to set up as a master. Equally uncertain is the term 'manufacturer'. John Edwards says that in that period 'manufacturer' meant 'journeyman weaver', but by the end of the century the simple term 'weaver' was used. He continues:

> It is likely that the change of name from manufacturer to weaver reflected a change in economic conditions for journeymen from being socially and economically almost the equal of the self-employed man to being one of a very large body entirely dependent for work upon the operations of large employer manufacturers. ('Norwich in the Eighteenth Century',

unpublished thesis, Norfolk Local History Library archives, 1972)

For at least the first half of the 19th century most weavers worked from their own homes, their employers, large or small, not needing a lot of space and only having houses or warehouses large enough to store the yarn, with space for a designer if they had one. Many of the designs were bought from freelance artists, only the larger manufacturers having their own design teams. The fringers and sewers could work either from home or in a part of the warehouse.

Working from home might be cramped and inconvenient but it meant that up to a point the weaver was his own boss, working as best suited him, so long as he got his work done to time. One of the most usual sights in the city was that of the weaver carrying his beam over his shoulder with his finished work back to the warehouse. There he would pick up fresh yarn, and a fresh design if he was to weave a new pattern, and take it back to his home.

This comparative freedom made for a very independent workman. A considerable number could at least read and write, and one of their great pleasures was discussion and argument about the political questions of the day. They could and did buy a copy of the weekly newspaper and the occasional magazine in a group, which was then read and mulled over in their slack moments. The majority of weavers lived in close proximity in the parishes near the river where the small cottages were closely grouped, making it easy for unofficial meetings. All during the 19th century trade ebbed and flowed with, at times, a considerable number of workmen unemployed and on short time, giving them opportunity for discussion. Their biggest worry was that new machinery might put even more of them out of work, and so any attempt by the larger manufacturers to introduce new ideas, such as the Jacquard machine, met with bitter resistance.

In the early 19th century the drawloom was in use, and it involved the necessity for an additional worker on the loom, the drawboy. It was his job to pull the cords which regulated the patterns to be woven. He was often very young, and as long as he was strong enough to pull the quite heavy cords he could be used. He was generally a son of the weaver. But, because of his youth, he could be inattentive and careless and was frequently very tired and bored. So although he was essential he was also a liability.

The Jacquard machine, patented in France in 1804, did away with the need for a drawboy. A further harness was mounted on top of the loom and the colours and the design were controlled by a strip of cards, each punched into holes which corresponded to the changes in the pattern.

From the point of view of the weaver the introduction of this new-fangled machine was not acceptable. The height of the extra harness precluded its use in a small cottage. The result would be that the workman would have to go and work in a bigger place, i.e., a factory, and the boy

A weaver working at home at his Jacquard machine. The perforated cards can be seen revolving above the web, doing away with the need for a drawboy. The weaver's wife is filling his bobbins for him. This engraving shows an ideal workshop which is much more spacious, comfortable and clean than the majority of those in Norwich, but it does have the birdcages for canaries which were so often seen in Norwich.

MACCLESFIELD MUSEUMS TRUST

54

would be out of a job. Even the shilling a week or so that he earned was of value to a family already near or on the breadline.

So strong was the feeling against the Jacquard that its first introduction was not until 1830, by the firm of Willett & Nephew. From a careful examination of the shawls in the collection at Strangers Hall Museum, it appears that the Jacquard never found favour with the shawl weavers, and that only one firm, that of Clabburn, Sons & Crisp, ever used it to any extent, and then not until about 1850. The Jacquard was in use for dress fabrics more than for shawls.

A shawl weaver was not paid by the day or the week but by the number of hanks of yarn he wove, the type of weave and the fineness of the weave, which meant that there was no such thing as an average wage. It depended on too many varying factors. Because of this difficulty, at Easter Quarter Sessions each year the Justices of the Peace, often manufacturers, carried out a review of rates paid, and authorised certain payments for the following year. In 1803 it was agreed that: 'if any dispute arises about the price to be paid for any new fancy articles, different from those the price of which is fixed by order of the Justices, a committee of masters and journeymen shall be appointed for the purpose of affixing the price' (*Norwich Mercury*, 30 July 1803).

As the times became more difficult for weaving these regulations were not observed, and things got so bad that in 1809 a draft case was sent to the Attorney General for his opinion regarding a jouneyman named Thomas Harmer who had been paid less than the wages laid down by the Justices. At the Michaelmas Quarter Sessions Harmer complained that John Thompson, a master and one of the signatories to the 1803 agreement, should have paid him £6. 3s. 9d. for shawl weaving but had only given him 4 guineas, therefore owing Harmer £1. 19s. 9d. At the hearing Thompson was fined 10 shillings but the Court held that they were not allowed by law to insist that he paid Harmer his arrears. Thompson argued that he was paying the same as the other masters and that none of

them could afford the wages agreed by the Magistrates. The Magistrates who sent the case to the Attorney General for advice were obviously on the side of the journeyman, saying: 'As the Evil is increasing and is a very serious one to the Journeymen the Magistrates are desirous of supporting them all they can particularly as their conduct has been remarkably temperate and proper.'

In this case the journeyman lost out all round. The Attorney General considered that by law the Justices could not penalise the master any more than 10 shillings. Harmer had had to take time off for the hearing, and his two witnesses who had vouched for Thompson's refusal to pay had also lost time and therefore money and they could not be recompensed. The Attorney General also said that in such cases a journeyman could apply to a Court of Conscience or a Court of Common Law for retribution, which, however, would mean that he would incur added expense and loss of yet more time. This opinion meant, in effect, that without some financial backing the workers were unable to fight loss of wages.

At the end of the case a hypothetical question was put to the Attorney General regarding the payment of wages in cash or 'Goods or Truck'. This shows that in 1809 'trucking' was not unknown in the textile world, but by the time of the worst recession in the trade, in 1826, it was rife. Trucking was used by unscrupulous overseers or managers in most trades in the 19th century and meant that instead of wages being paid in cash they were paid either with vouchers which could only be exchanged for goods at shops owned by the firm, or were paid in actual goods, often unwanted by the worker, who then had to sell these goods to get the money in order to buy the food needed by himself and his family.

According to letters in the *Norwich Mercury* (October 1826), the 'goods' in lieu of cash appear to have been unwanted ends of lines which the manufacturers were only too pleased to get rid of at a very high price. One letter, written by the Committee of Weavers and signed by William Press, said that the weavers were not allowed to take their wages in 'lawful coin of the realm' but it must be in such articles as 'blankets, of the coarser sort at 3/- per lb, fustian at 20d per yard (valued by impartial judges at 13d per yard), sarsnets 4/- per yard (valued 2/8d) . . . shawls with fillover borders at the enormous sum of £4 (valued at 70/-) . . .'. After this, 'those articles must be turned into money at some price and generally at such a reduction as causes his real earnings to be reduced to less than half, and very often (notwithstanding he is in danger of being put into prison for hawking without a licence) he is not able to get a market even at that price . . . then to the pawnbroker . . .'. The letter written by the Committee of Weavers ends: 'We trust that when the case shall be altered, that every weaver will never submit to such tyrants, but will leave them one and all. We have the magistrates on our side to whom we return our sincerest thanks.'

It would be interesting to know what proportion of the many manufacturers engaged in these unpleasant practices. Probably not many, but enough to be extremely unsettling to the weavers.

It generally happens that when everything in trade is going smoothly, nothing much is reported about it in the newspapers, and this was as true in the 19th century as today. The result is that we only hear of wages when there is a call for reduction and very seldom when there is an increase.

It was between 1822 and 1826 that the trade was at its most difficult and there was an only-to-be-expected call for lower wages. In a long article in the *Norwich Mercury* of 13 July 1822, it was stated by the manufacturers that Yorkshire goods were cheaper. Norwich could not compete, therefore prices, which meant wages, must go down. In the same article, the Committee of Journeyman Weavers issued a statement saying that in 1809 wages had been raised, but that the present proposal would be to send them down to the pre-1809 rate. The statement went on to say: 'Has he [the weaver] now more than is sufficient? That is the real question.' It then continued with a hypothetical family of a man, wife and four children with the man weaving a middle-rate bombazine (which was not paid as well as shawl weaving):

> Working 12 hours a day in 3 weeks he can weave 2 pieces for £2. 5s. 0d. which is 15/- per week. His wife will fill his bobbins but his outgoing for a week, and this for 6 people will be as follows:

Winding on, twisting on, shuttle, pickers and card	6
Rent	2/6
Firing, the year round	1/3
Meat 3/4 lb per day	2/2
Bread	4/0
Flour 1/2 a stone	1/2
Beer 1 pt per day	1/6
Butter 1/2 a pint	8
Cheese 1/2 a lb	4
Milk 1 pt per day	9
Tea 1 oz	5
Sugar 1/2 a lb	4
Sauce	1/0
Soap, candles and oil, year round	1/0
Salt, pepper, vinegar and sundries	4
For bedding, clothing etc.	1/0
[Total expenditure]	18/11
Income	15/-

The example concluded with the cry: 'There is 3/11 more going out than coming in – let anyone judge!'

The weaver might also have been lucky enough to have an allotment. These were recognised officially in 1850 but had been in precarious existence for many years before. As they were set up to 'feed the poor' it was likely that weavers could have benefited, but whether they did or not is not known.

Also in 1822 there was a split among the manufacturers between those who thought a reduction of wages essential and those who thought they could pull through the recession without it. To make the weavers' position clear, 'The Humble Address of the Committee of Journeyman Weavers

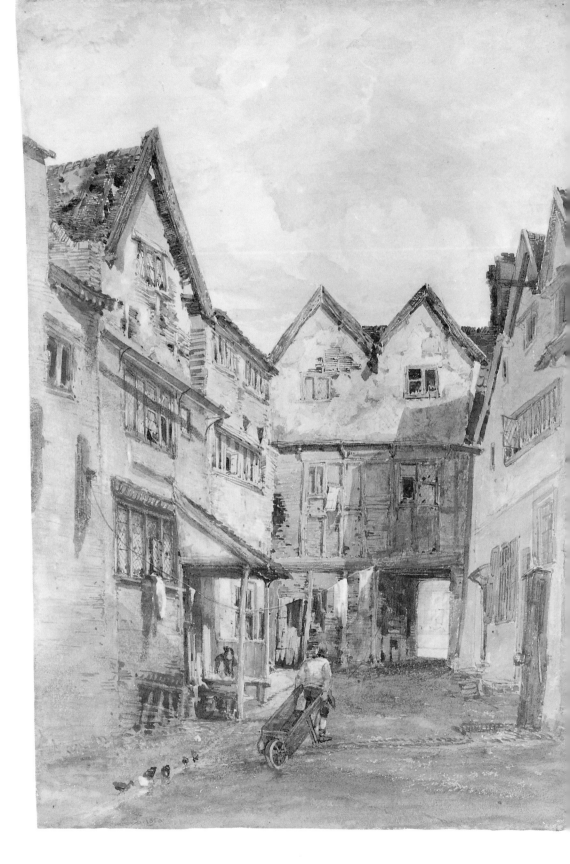

Old Yard in Oak Street, Norwich *(1850), by Thomas Lound. Oak Street is in the area near the River Wensum where most of the weavers, their families and those of the ancillary trades lived and worked. The watercolour shows the long weaver's windows in the houses, and, also, how little light could get into some of the windows. On a dark, dull day in winter a candle would be needed all day.*
CASTLE MUSEUM, NORWICH

of the City of Norwich to the General Manufacturers' was published (*Norwich Mercury*, 27 July 1822). This asked that another meeting of manufacturers might be convened and that a deputation of journeymen might be allowed to attend to put their case. From the address it was obvious that some of the weavers had become extremely belligerent against some manufacturers.

A photograph of James Churchyard at his loom. The date is uncertain but is possibly 1913.
BRIDEWELL MUSEUM, NORWICH

In 1826 the recession in the weaving trade was at its worst, and not only in Norwich. Spitalfields in London was also affected. In Norwich 3,000–4,000 weavers met in Chapel Field on 5 August 1826 and the whole matter of reduction of wages was discussed again. They harked back to the 1822 resolution which had said that there would be no reduction but pointed out that some manufacturers had got round this by trucking and by the even more disliked method of sending work out into the surrounding villages, especially Wymondham, where the weavers were willing to work for reduced rates. This problem had been boiling up for some years and with lack of food, lack of work and lack of money the Norwich weavers were ready for battle. In one case, seeing the carrier's cart sent from Forncett standing against an Elm Hill workshop, taking in work and bringing out yarn, they took the horse out of the cart, destroyed the cart and its contents and broke all the windows in the factory. They visited the pubs from which the carriers' carts started and searched the carts and took any materials for work to the Guildhall. Mr Purdy's warehouse in Peacock Street was also damaged, at Mr Willett's factory they demolished not only the windows but also the frames in the lower rooms and at a factory in St John Timberhill, four storeys high, they broke all the windows. The Riot Act was read in the Market and the Dragoons (Scots Greys) were sent for, while special constables guarded the rest of the manufactories. On the following day the manufacturers agreed not to send work out of the city while there was any unemployment.

The census of 1851 makes clear the fact that in the shawl trade the weaver was only one man of a large team. He was not even the most important man and he worked in the middle of the team. There were vital jobs without which he could not have started his work, and there were also other jobs after he had finished. It was teamwork which counted.

While the census is excellent evidence for existence of the different jobs, the numbers for some are questionable, as the enumerators, who were not fully conversant with the terms of the trade, would not have performed their task with accuracy.

In 1851 in the various parishes, mostly near the river, there were about 2,500 weavers, which included all the textile workers – not only the shawl weavers. The weavers were enumerated in various professional categories (with individual weavers occupying more than one): 684 are just named as 'weavers', so it is not known on what they were working; 350 are handloom weavers; 403 handloom silk weavers; 500 silk weavers and only 60 worsted weavers. There were 155 mixed weavers, presumably working with silk and wool or silk and cotton, and sadly 117 paupers, 'formerly weavers'. It is not clear where the Jacquard weavers came in this list. There is no mention of them at all, so possibly as the Jacquard had been accepted by 1851 they came into the section of 684 weavers.

Drawboys are not mentioned in the 1851 census, though they must still have been necessary in some cases. The following fourteen jobs are enumerated and pertain specifically to the shawl trade:

Borderer: a weaver of the narrow edge borders which were sewn on to shawls.

Cleaner: meaning not entirely clear.

Clipper or cropper: the man using special shears, who clipped all the loose threads from the back of the design, making the shawl much lighter in weight as well as tidier. There was also a machine, over which the shawl was passed, which clipped.

Dresser: the man who dressed the warp. In Scotland, according to David Gilmour in *The Pen Folk* it was the weaver himself, but in Norwich it might be a man skilled at this very tricky and time-consuming job; as well as the weaver.

Filler: probably the bobbin filler, often the weaver's wife.

Fringer: probably worked in the manufacturer's house or factory where the shawl would be finished, though one firm only made fringes.

Jacquard cutter: probably the most taxing job of all. The man who punched the holes in the cards for the design on point paper prepared by the pattern drawer. On the cutter and the lasher depended all the accuracy or otherwise of the finished design.

Lasher: this could be the man who lashed the Jacquard cards together in the correct order, or, on the drawloom, the 'flower lasher' who read the design and put all the cords together for the drawboy to pull. In fact, the same job for two different types of loom.

Maker: possibly a synonym for weaver.

Mounter: the man who mounted the harness on the loom.

Printer: generally a block printer.

Sewer: a girl who sewed on the borders and also the fringe.

Washer: the shawls had to be washed after weaving in order to get rid of the size with which the warp had been dressed.

Worker: possibly a synonym for weaver.

This list, though long, leaves out the most important man of all, the designer. He might be in-house or freelance, local or from London or some other large centre. A few were local artists such as Obadiah Short or John Funnell, but of the rest we know virtually nothing. They are seldom named, but on looking at a large number of shawls it becomes possible to pick out several by their 'handwriting'. They leave individual quirks and one can spot their idiosyncracies. Would that we knew more about them.

It is not easy to find out a great deal about the lives of individual weavers though we know a certain amount about two of them.

William Armes was a weaver who lived in Barrack Street. He was a competent workman who wove a reversible shawl now in the Museum (cat. no. 127). His great niece remembers, as a small child, watching him carry his beam with his finished work on it, to his master's in Saint Clements Alley. At this time this must have been the firm of C & F Bolingbroke. However, in the census he is classed as a mariner. Having two trades was not unusual and it was comparatively simple in Norfolk. The East Coast herring fleet fished close to the shore from September to December each year, and it was quite normal for men in a trade with seasonal fluctuations to work on the boats for two or three months. In a good season they could earn enough to help keep their families through a bad time ashore.

James Churchyard worked as a weaver all his life and died in 1913. He epitomises many weavers who did not always work for one master. James certainly worked for Grouts, for Middleton & Answorth and also for Clabburn, Sons & Crisp. His great niece possesses fourteen of his pieces, of which the Museum now has four (cat. nos 67–70). They are very varied, probably reflecting the type of shawl made by his employer of the time. He seems to have worked chiefly on the Jacquard. The shawls owned by the Museum include one of fine organza in black and grey, brocaded with pink roses at infrequent intervals (no. 70). The very light silk is ruined by a heavy black woollen fringe knotted on, which might well be a later addition. Another is completely different, being of a thick soft wool in an irregular chevron stripe (no. 69). It is warp printed to give a cloud effect. Yet another is of silk twill in small checks of tobacco, fawn and cream (no. 68). No. 67 is one of which we have several examples, made for Clabburn, Sons & Crisp, of dense flowers and medallion patterns in horizontal stripes. These very different types of shawl show the versatility of the Jacquard loom in that one man can weave in so many different threads as well as styles.

The Norwich weaver was nothing if not accomplished. He might well be, and was, obstinate, averse to change and independent, but he was also a competent and often brilliant weaver who loved his home, his tiny garden and his Norwich canary and produced some wonderful shawls.

Catalogue

PART TWO

TURNOVER SHAWLS AND CHINESE ARCHITECTURAL DESIGNS

The collection includes nine turnover shawls, of which five come into the category called Norwich Chinese Architectural. A turnover is one where only the borders are important. They are always sewn onto a plain centre and have two adjoining sides sewn on one way with the other two reversed. When the shawl is folded diagonally the borders, placed with one pair above the other pair, all show their right sides and make a V-shape on the back of the wearer.

The style of design called Chinese Architectural has clear colours with a precise pattern of motifs resembling chinoiserie. The only known occurrence of this particular type of design in Norwich is on turnover shawls. This points to one particular manufacturer and one designer – both unknown.

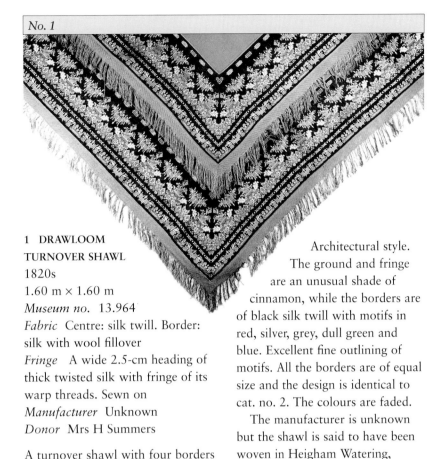

No. 1

1 DRAWLOOM TURNOVER SHAWL
1820s
1.60 m × 1.60 m
Museum no. 13.964
Fabric Centre: silk twill. Border: silk with wool fillover
Fringe A wide 2.5-cm heading of thick twisted silk with fringe of its warp threads. Sewn on
Manufacturer Unknown
Donor Mrs H Summers

A turnover shawl with four borders of equal width, designed in Chinese Architectural style. The ground and fringe are an unusual shade of cinnamon, while the borders are of black silk twill with motifs in red, silver, grey, dull green and blue. Excellent fine outlining of motifs. All the borders are of equal size and the design is identical to cat. no. 2. The colours are faded.

The manufacturer is unknown but the shawl is said to have been woven in Heigham Watering, Norwich.

2 DRAWLOOM TURNOVER SHAWL
1820s
1.60 m × 1.60 m
Museum no. 199.967.4
Fabric Centre: silk warp, wool weft; twill. Border: wool fillover with some silk on silk twill
Fringe Silk threads from narrow heading. Sewn on
Manufacturer Unknown
Donor Mrs O J Miller

A turnover shawl with two wide and two narrow borders, designed in the Chinese Architectural style. In contrast to cat. no. 1 the ground colour and that of the border are the same – black. Because the weaving threads are of different thicknesses to those of no. 1 it is not immediately apparent that the border design is identical.

The manufacturer is unknown but the shawl is said to have been woven in Heigham Watering, Norwich.

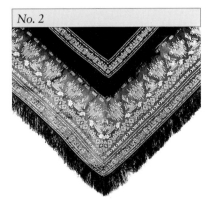

No. 2

No. 3

3 DRAWLOOM TURNOVER SHAWL
1820s
1.56 m × 1.56 m
Museum no. 830.967.2
Fabric Centre: silk twill. Border: silk with wool fillover
Fringe Plain unknotted silk on heading. Sewn on
Manufacturer Unknown
Donor Bought

This turnover shawl has two wide and two narrow borders. The ground is cream with clear red, blue and yellow motifs. The design is Chinese Architectural with the addition of an occasional formal pine with a serrated edge.

No. 4

4 DRAWLOOM TURNOVER SHAWL
1820s
1.42 m × 1.42 m
Museum no. 333.984
Fabric Centre: silk twill. Border: silk with wool fillover
Fringe Thin silk from heading. Sewn on
Manufacturer Unknown
Donor Friends of Norwich Museums

This petite, dainty shawl is not quite in the Chinese Architectural style but its angular and small design follows the same principles. It has a cream centre and four equal sized borders. Three bands of the border are made as one. The outer 2.5 cm are cream with small red and blue sprays; the middle 5 cm are caramel with blue and white flowers and red leaves; the inner 2 cm have a blue serpentine stem and leaves with red and white flowers, on a mushroom-coloured background.

No. 5

5 DRAWLOOM TURNOVER SHAWL
Late 1820s
1.60 m × 1.60 m
Museum no. 151.946
Fabric Centre: silk twill. Border: silk
Fringe Silk strands from heading. Sewn on
Manufacturer Unknown
Donor Mrs Matthews

This turnover shawl has two wide (25-cm) and two narrow (5-cm) borders. The design is very angular, of exotic flowers in large motifs with sprays of foliage between, and using red, yellow and green on a black ground.

No. 6

6 DRAWLOOM TURNOVER SHAWL
1825–30
1.45 m × 1.45 m
Museum no. 191.980.1
Fabric Centre: silk warp, wool weft; twill. Border: wool fillover with alternate motifs in silk
Fringe Narrow heading with thick short silk fringe. Sewn on
Manufacturer Unknown
Donor Mrs Faircloth

This is an unusual turnover and is possibly an experimental shawl. The centre is black and the four borders are of equal size (11 cm). Their designs are of upright pines predominantly in green and gold alternating with fancifully scrolled triangular motifs in crimson silk.

No. 7

7 DRAWLOOM TURNOVER SHAWL
1830s
1.55 m × 1.55 m
Museum no. 217.977.1
Fabric Centre: silk twill. Border: silk with wool fillover
Fringe Silk threads from the central woven fabric. Sewn on all round
Manufacturer Unknown
Donor Miss W E Attoe

This is a rather flowery form of Chinese Architectural. The borders are all the same size and have a ground of either light or dark brown with crimson, blue and yellow motifs. The weaving is very fine.

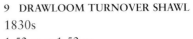

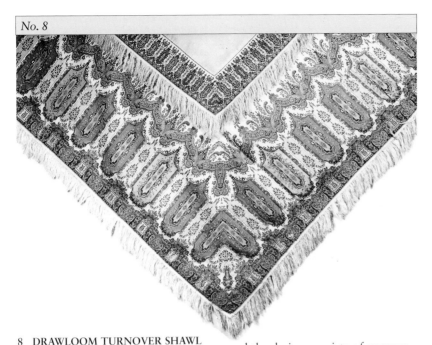

8 DRAWLOOM TURNOVER SHAWL
1835–40
1.57 m × 1.57 m
Museum no. 96.944
Fabric Centre: wool twill. Border:
silk twill with wool fillover
Fringe Silk from heading. Sewn on
Manufacturer Unknown
Donor Mrs Row

There are two very wide (38-cm)
and two narrow (7-cm) borders

and the design consists of narrow
rectangular medallions going to a
point at the top with a curved
base. They are alternately
cinnamon, red and blue and are
Chinese Architectural in style. The
shawl was exhibited in Edinburgh
in 1962 as an Edinburgh type but
it was given to the Museum in
1944 as a Norwich type and
resembles other Norwich shawls.

9 DRAWLOOM TURNOVER SHAWL
1830s
1.52 m × 1.52 m
Museum no. 639.965
Fabric Ground: fine wool; twill.
Border: fine silk with wool fillover
Fringe Narrow heading with thick
short silk threads. Sewn on
Manufacturer Possibly Schickle,
Towler & Campin
Donor Mrs H Bryan

A very unusual turnover shawl.
The centre is black and there are
two wide borders and two narrow,
reversed. The narrow borders have
angular sparse sprigs woven on the
straight of the fabric. The two wide
borders with a design of angular
pines and sprigs are woven with
the silk on the bias. This must be
an experiment in technique as
below the border design are woven
lines which are parallel with the
edge of the shawl. The colours are
yellow, green, red and blue, with
the motifs outlined with simple
yellow stitches. It was possibly
made by Schickle, Towler,
Campin & Co. as the design
closely resembles their registered
design no. 8361.

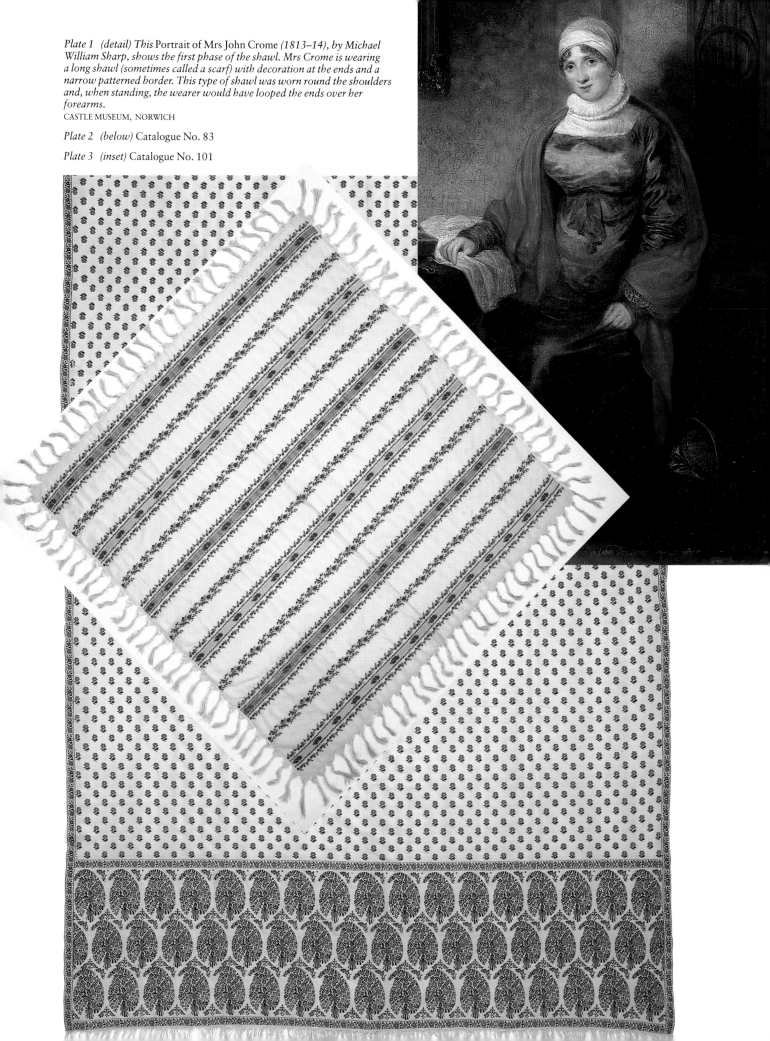

Plate 1 (detail) This Portrait of Mrs John Crome (1813–14), by Michael William Sharp, shows the first phase of the shawl. Mrs Crome is wearing a long shawl (sometimes called a scarf) with decoration at the ends and a narrow patterned border. This type of shawl was worn round the shoulders and, when standing, the wearer would have looped the ends over her forearms.
CASTLE MUSEUM, NORWICH

Plate 2 (below) Catalogue No. 83

Plate 3 (inset) Catalogue No. 101

Plate 4 *(left)* Catalogue No. 74
Plate 5 *(below)* Catalogue No. 87
Plate 6 *(facing page)* Catalogue No. 32

Plate 7 (detail) Departing for the Promenade (Will You Go Out With Me, Fido?) (1859) by Alfred Stevens. A mid-19th-century shawl, this is a different shape and type from that in Plate 1. The wide rectangle is completely covered by the design, and the fullness of the clothes shows off the colours and patterns to the best advantage.

PHILADELPHIA MUSEUM OF ART: THE WP WILSTACH COLLECTION, BEQUEST OF ANNA H WILSTACH

Plate 8 Catalogue No. 122

Plate 9 Catalogue No. 106

Plate 10 *(far left, facing page)* Catalogue No. 99 *(detail)*

Plate 11 *(facing page)* Catalogue No. 31

Plate 12 *(detail)* The Awakening Conscience *(1853), by William Holman Hunt. The last phase of the shawl. In spite of the compromising position in which the woman finds herself, this painting accurately prefigures the way in which the shawl was worn – by middle and upper-class women alike – shortly before its fall from fashion in the 1860s. The fullness of the skirt has been pulled to the back, forming the bustle, and the shawl has been folded and tied round the hips.*

TATE GALLERY, LONDON

Plate 13 Catalogue No. 57

Plate 14   (left) Catalogue No. 46 (*detail*)

Plate 15   Catalogue No. 47

SHAWLS BY TOWLER & CAMPIN

Towler & Campin Printed Shawls

From 1842 the designs of printed and woven shawls could be registered at the Public Record Office and the firm of Towler & Campin took full advantage of this. During the period of either three or six months a design which had been registered could not be used by anyone else. This gave manufacturers a chance to get a newly designed shawl on the market before other places copied the design. Towler & Campin used the possibilities of registration more than any other in Norwich. The company also had many changes of name. In 1830–6 it was Shickle, Towler & Campin; 1836–41 Towler & Shickle; 1842–5 Towler, Campin, Shickle & Matthews; 1843–51 Towler, Campin & Co; for 1851–62 the name is not known but is likely to be Towler, Campin, Monteith & Co; in 1862–9 it was Towler, Rowling & Allen and in 1872 Towler & Allen. The dates given here can only be considered as approximate, as they vary with different authorities (see the introductory note to the Appendix). For ease of reference, the company is usually referred to as Towler & Campin.

The shawls printed by this firm were mostly of a closely woven twilled silk leno (gauze) with a few being of a closely woven twilled silk. The leno shawls have an idiosyncracy which has not been found in the work of any other firm anywhere, which makes for easy identification. About 3 cm in from the edge there is a band of thick ribbed weaving approximately 6 cm wide, which protects the fine leno from tearing. The width of the ribbed weaving varies slightly according to the size of the shawl.

10 BLOCK PRINTED SHAWL
*c.*1845
3.34 m × 1.70 m
Museum no. 191.970.1
Fabric Silk leno
Fringe Cream silk 12 cm long, cross-knotted
Manufacturer Towler, Campin, Shickle & Matthews
Donor Miss C Oakley

A shawl with wide alternate stripes of maroon and cream which are edged with scrolled sprays. There are arabesques of the same colour all over.

No. 10

11 BLOCK PRINTED SHAWL
*c.*1845
2.06 m × 2.06 m
Museum no. 256.966.1
Fabric Wool twill
Fringe Warp threads tightly twisted
Manufacturer Probably Towler & Campin
Donor Unknown

A very unusual shawl but strongly resembling a registered design of Towler & Campin (no. 30442 PRO). The design consists of flowered bands forming interlocking quadrilles on a densely flower-printed cream ground. As the fabric is a slightly hairy wool the colours are very subdued, but include muted greens, blues and mauves.

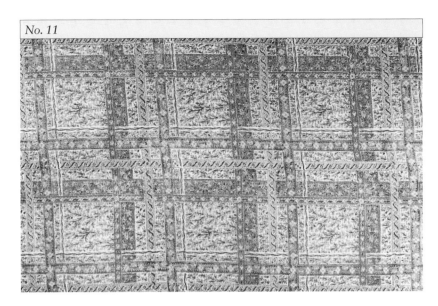

No. 11

12 BLOCK PRINTED SHAWL
*c.*1850
3.63 m × 2.03 m
Museum no. 560.973
Fabric Silk leno
Fringe Silk threads cross-knotted on ends of shawl
Manufacturer Towler, Campin & Co
Donor Mrs M Bowles

A plain-centred shawl with a continuous border all round consisting of mop-headed flowers, other plants, scrolls, flowers and leaves. The fringe and edge of the border are beetroot colour, but the ground effect is of warm colouring with some cool aqua blues, all on cream.

No. 12

No. 13

13 BLOCK PRINTED SHAWL

1850

1.94 m × 0.61 m

Museum no. 403.975

Fabric Silk leno

Fringe Long strands knotted on

Manufacturer Towler & Campin
(no. 67158 PRO)

Donor Bought

A cream long scarf with a border
all round of upright geometric

pines clasped at their base by a
rococo vase. Between the pines is
an angular sprig. The general effect
of the colouring is pinkish.

The printing is of low quality,
which suggests that poor printing
by this firm was done in their own
works but that the very good work
seen in some of their shawls was
done by the firm of Swaisland at
Crayford in Kent.

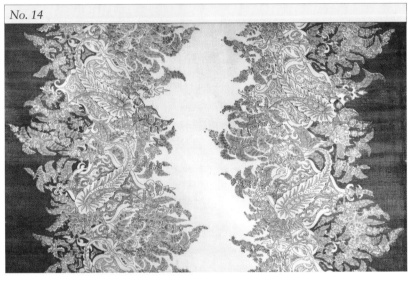

No. 14

14 BLOCK PRINTED SHAWL

*c.*1851

1.90 m × 1.90 m

Museum no. 147.963

Fabric Silk leno

Fringe 10 cm cross-knotted on

Manufacturer Towler & Campin

Donor Mrs Percival

This shawl has alternate wavy
stripes of cream and maroon with
stripes of pine, leaf and flower
decoration overlapping both
colours. There is a lot of hatching
in the design, generally used to
suggest the twill weave of the more
expensive woven designs.

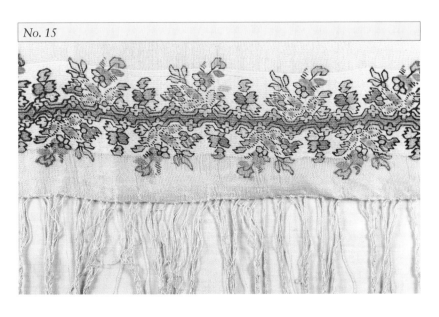

No. 15

15 BLOCK PRINTED SHAWL

1851

1.02 m × 1.02 m

Museum no. 751.967.1

Fabric Silk leno

Fringe 10 cm cream silk knotted
on

Manufacturer Towler & Campin
(no. 75613 PRO)

Donor Mrs Jarman

A small light summer shawl with a
narrow border. The border consists
of a 10-cm band of diagonally
arranged pink and sulphur-yellow
flowers on a solid mauve centre
stripe.

16 BLOCK PRINTED SHAWL
1851
1.98 m × 1.82 m
Museum no. 1993.155.2
Fabric Heavy twilled silk
Fringe Black silk knotted on
Manufacturer Towler & Campin
(no. 75614 PRO)
Donor Miss Jean Gowing

Bright stripes of exotic flowers extend into the black centre of the shawl. The colours are unusually bright: red, yellow, mauve, blue and green. The outer edge of the border has a series of 'chandelier' swags which seem to be a trade mark of this unknown designer.

17 BLOCK PRINTED SHAWL
1851
3.45 m × 1.74 m
Museum no. 843.967.1
Fabric Silk leno
Fringe 15 cm long silk threads knotted on
Manufacturer Towler & Campin
(nos 75614 and 75612 PRO)
Donor Mrs Hepworth

This item shows clearly how registered designs could be used in various ways. Design no. 75612 is a swirling frond on a double boat-shaped base, seen in cat. nos 19 and 20. Here it is used as the top of the border while the base is formed of design no. 75614 (cat. no. 16).

There are no pines in any of these four shawls and the colours are much the same with reds and mauves, a little green and sulphur yellow.

No. 16

No. 17

70

No. 18

18 BLOCK PRINTED SHAWL
1851
1.72 m × 1.72 m
Museum no. 120.988
Fabric Silk leno
Fringe Twisted silk knotted on
Manufacturer Towler, Campin &
Co (nos 75614 and 82716 PRO)
Donor Bought

A shawl with a combination of two registered designs. It is unusual in that the edge and the fringe are of the brilliant Norwich red, while the rest of the ground is cream. The colouring of the whole gives a hot impression with much red and mauve and a little yellow, green and blue.

No. 19

19 BLOCK PRINTED SHAWL
1851
1.72 m × 1.72 m
Museum no. 670.971
Fabric Very fine silk twill
Fringe Long silk threads knotted on all round
Manufacturer Towler & Campin (no. 75612 PRO)
Donor Lt Col the Revd C P Hines, OBE

The same design as no. 20. The outside design is on bright red and the inner on the main colour, white.

20   BLOCK PRINTED SHAWL
1851
1.72 m × 1.72 m
Museum no. 185.986.1
Fabric Silk leno
Fringe 12 cm silk knotted on all round
Manufacturer Towler & Campin (no. 75612 PRO)
Donor Mrs K Sapey

This shawl has the swirling design used in different ways in four shawls in this collection (see nos 17, 18 and 19). Here it is used twice, once facing out on a beetroot ground and then reversed and facing in on the main cream ground. The colours in this shawl are restricted to reds, cream, light green and sulphur.

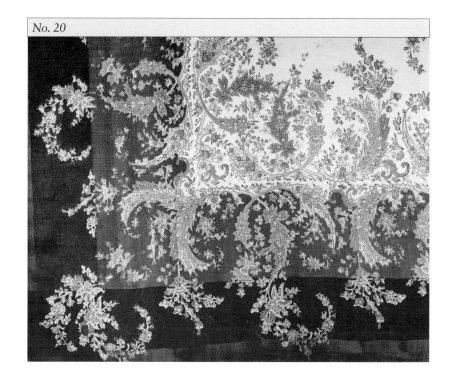
No. 20

21   BLOCK PRINTED SHAWL
1852
1.60 m × 1.60 m
Museum no. 234.971
Fabric Silk leno
Fringe 15 cm silk threads cross-knotted on
Manufacturer Towler & Campin (no. 82717 PRO)
Donor Mrs Allan

The donor states that originally the main colour was a bright cerise on a cream ground, but after washing it became beetroot on a pink ground. There is a beetroot wavy border stripe with swags, sprays and tendrils overlapping the stripe.

No. 21

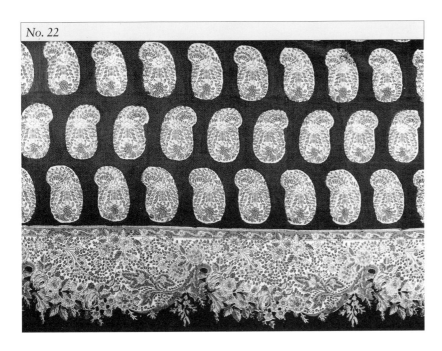

No. 22

22 BLOCK PRINTED SHAWL
1853
1.60 m × 1.60 m
Museum no. 675.971
Fabric Silk twill
Fringe Black silk knotted on all round
Manufacturer Towler & Campin. Centre: no. 82715 PRO. Border: no. 82713 PRO
Donor Mrs Daniells

This is one of the shawls where two designs have been amalgamated. The centre is black with stubby small pines in staggered rows, each row facing in the opposite direction. The border contains roses, forget-me-nots and other unrecognisable flowers and leaves. It is resist dyed, leaving a white ground with red, green and pale blue on it.

No. 23

23 BLOCK PRINTED SHAWL
1830–50
1.60 m × 1.40 m
Museum no. 821.967.2
Fabric Silk leno
Fringe Black silk knotted on
Manufacturer Towler & Campin
Donor Miss C G Baker

This is a mourning shawl and as such is absolutely plain with no relief. As there is no pattern the band of ribbed weaving shows up very clearly.

Towler & Campin Woven Shawls

Of the seven firms in Norwich to register their designs with the PRO, Towler & Campin registered the greatest number. Consequently from 1842 we have a record of some of their woven designs (they did not register every one) which makes it possible to identify a number of their shawls. It is also possible, from the general 'handwriting' of the designer, to identify some prior to 1842, but these are always noted as 'probably'.

No. 24

24 DRAWLOOM SHAWL
1840s
1.77 m × 1.74 m
Museum no. 226.972.21
Fabric Ground: silk warp, wool weft; twill. Fillover: silk and wool
Fringe Single strands of twisted cream wool 10 cm long, knotted on all round
Manufacturer Probably Towler & Campin
Donor Miss D J Miller

A beautiful shawl with a cream ground. It has a design with a border of dense pines intricately entwined. These merge into exotic flower sprays which form a circle round a plain centre. The weaving is superb and the design particularly well managed especially at the corners. The colours are red, green, pale blue, yellow and black.

This shawl is likely to be by Towler & Campin though the design is not registered. It may well pre-date registration and be late 1830s or early 1840s.

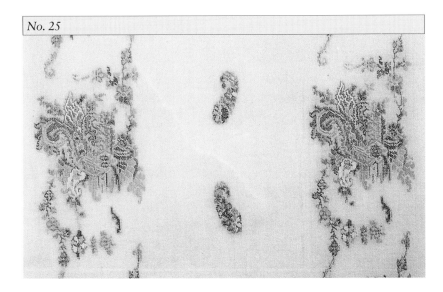

No. 25

25 DRAWLOOM SHAWL
Mid-1840s
1.52 m × 1.37 m
Museum no. 93.949
Fabric Ground: silk warp, wool weft; twill. Fillover: wool
Fringe Long silk threads knotted on all round in groups
Manufacturer Possibly Towler & Campin
Donor Miss Moffitt

This is a much washed and worn shawl and probably lower-priced than most. It is cut from yardage and has no black or dark colour in the design. The design is one which, in the idea though not in the detail, was much used. It consists of exotic flower clusters with foliage coming from an urn or motif. The clusters are in stripes between which are small single isolated pines (see no. 26).

No. 26

26 DRAWLOOM SHAWL
Mid-1840s
1.52 m × 1.37 m
Museum no. 40.942.2
Fabric Ground: silk warp, wool weft; twill. Fillover: wool
Fringe Long, sparse silk knotted in groups
Manufacturer Possibly Towler & Campin
Donor Mrs Spurrell

A shawl resembling no. 25 and obviously from the same manufacturer. Again there are no dark colours or black. The design is of bunches of exotic flowers in stripes, with a mirror-image and tiny flower and leaf forms between the rows. The colour effect is of red and yellow with green on cream.

The fabric is cut from yardage and the edges are turned in and run.

27 DRAWLOOM SHAWL
1840s
1.60 m × 1.60 m
Museum no. 103.977.23
Fabric Ground: wool twill.
Fillover: wool. Cut from yardage
Fringe Silk strands from narrow
heading with nine forming a single
knot. Sewn on
Manufacturer Probably Towler &
Campin
Donors The estate of Miss E Press

Stripes of exotic red, white and
blue flowers, with green leaves
from urn-like motifs, alternate with
stripes of small sprays. Each
tendril, leaf or flower is outlined
with a single stitch, usually of gold.
Although the outlining of motifs is
common at this time, the edging is
clearer and more obvious than
usual. The ground colour is black.

No. 27

28 DRAWLOOM SHAWL
1842
1.52 m × 1.52 m
Museum no. 123.947.5
Fabric Ground: silk twill. Fillover:
wool and a little silk
Fringe Long strands of cream silk
from heading with a single knot
every 5 cm. Sewn on
Manufacturer Towler & Campin
(no. 5332 PRO)
Donor Mrs Reeve

The shawl has a mirror-image
design. These are not always easy
to detect at first glance. This one
consists of an all-over trailing
design with sparse sprays at
intervals, without pines. On a
cream ground are sparse dark
green, red, pink and yellow sprays
with black, very angular, stems.

No. 28

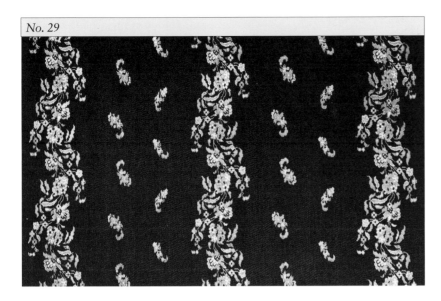

No. 29

29 DRAWLOOM SHAWL
1843
1.47 m × 1.47 m
Museum no. 749.968.2
Fabric Wool; twill. Cut from yardage
Fringe Narrow heading, with black silk knotted in groups. Sewn on
Manufacturer Towler & Campin (no. 8361 PRO)
Donor Maddermarket Theatre Wardrobe

Stripes of continuous floral pattern, 7 cm wide, alternate with spaced pine-shaped sprigs in two different motifs, one 2.5 cm high, the other 1.5 cm. The black ground has pink, blue, green, white and a little yellow on it.

No. 30

30 DRAWLOOM SHAWL
1843
1.20 m × 1.20 m
Museum no. 270.969
Fabric Ground: silk warp, wool weft; twill. Fillover: wool. Cut from yardage
Fringe Heavy silk with narrow heading. Eight groups tied with one knot. Sewn on
Manufacturer Towler & Campin (no. 6268 PRO)
Donor Bought

Another design with a mirror image. All over are medium pines joined by trailing stems, leaves and exotic flowers. Red, pink, green and yellow with black stems on cream ground. A very light design.

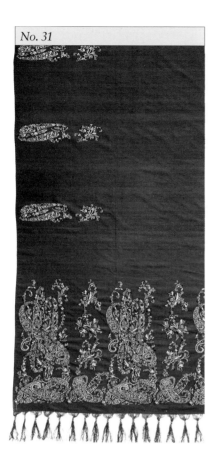

No. 31

No. 32

31 DRAWLOOM SHAWL
1844
3.22 m × 1.62 m
Museum no. 542.972
Fabric Ground: silk warp and wool weft; twill. Fillover: wool with some silk
Fringe Narrow heading with groups of silk threads in single knot at ends. Sewn on
Manufacturer Towler, Campin, Shickle & Matthews (no. 21398 PRO)
Donor Mrs Wayne

The striking colour of this shawl is that known as Norwich Red. Until the late 1830s (the date is uncertain) it had been impossible to dye wool and silk exactly the same colour so the ground colour was cream where the threads were mixed, or if a colour was needed plain silk was used. Close examination of this shawl reveals that even in the 1840s the dyeing firm of Wm Stark (see chapter 7) had not perfected the match of colour but it is very close. The end borders have diagonal twisted pines intertwined with foliage (the beginning of convolution). There are no side borders but every 30 cm there is a double pine surmounted by a spray pointing to the centre. The sides are hemmed as there is no selvedge.

The shawl belonged to Mrs Buxton, grandmother of the donor.

32 DRAWLOOM SHAWL
1845
1.60 m × 1.60 m
Museum no. 1994.66
Fabric Ground: silk warp, wool weft; twill. Fillover: wool
Fringe Cream silk knotted onto a narrow heading. Sewn on
Manufacturer Towler & Campin (no. 25053 PRO)
Donor Costume and Textile Association

This shawl has a mirror-image design, and is divided into four by densely packed sprays of exotic flowers. In the four compartments are lighter trailing sprays. In each corner of the shawl and in the centre of each side is a 6-cm-square medallion with a strong yellow ground in which is a small nearly symmetrical design. Mostly red, pink and mauve with green and a little yellow and blue. Black stems, all on cream.

No. 33

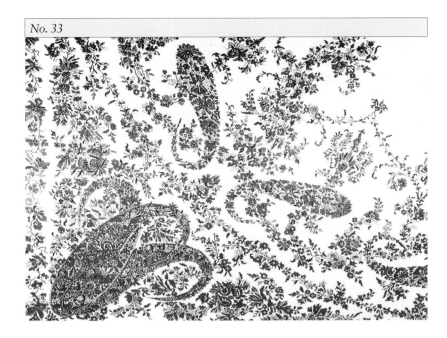

No. 34

33 DRAWLOOM SHAWL
1846
1.79 m × 1.64 m
Museum no. 115.985
Fabric Ground: silk twill. Fillover:
wool
Fringe Strands of heavy twisted
silk 15 cm long from narrow
heading. Sewn on
Manufacturer Towler, Campin &
Co (no. 36911 PRO)
Donor Colonel Tillett

This shawl has a colour scheme
which is much darker in tone than
usual for one with a cream ground.
It is chiefly dark green, dark red
and dark blue lightened with pink
and beige. The design is heavy at
the corners with overlapping pines,
but eventually forms a garlanded
circle leaving a plain cream centre.
Unusually, there is woven hatching
on some motifs which is generally
seen on printed shawls simulating
weave, and the outside edges of the
pines are defined in a one-stitch
chequer board pattern.

34 DRAWLOOM SHAWL
1869–70
3.10 m × 1.67 m
Museum no. 451.966.1
Fabric Ground: silk twill. Fillover:
rather rough wool
Fringe Mostly missing. Originally
warp threads
Manufacturer Towler, Rowling &
Allen
Donor Mrs Teather

When Queen Victoria visited
Norwich in 1869 she was given a
shawl woven by Towler, Rowling
& Allen. It appears that when the
city bought shawls as gifts to
royalty, although complete secrecy
was supposed to be kept as to the
design, several were made,
sometimes differing slightly. This
one was given to the Museum by
Abel Towler's granddaughter, who
said that her grandfather had had
this one made for his daughter,
although he was not allowed to.
However, the Museum has a half
shawl of exactly the same design
but a different colour, and another
with only the slightest deviation!

The silk ground of this shawl is
a strong red for one half and a
strong blue for the other. The
design is of palms, urns, pines and
falling sprays in muted shades
76 cm deep at the ends and 38 cm
at the sides. A 5-cm flowery design
covers the central meeting of red
and blue.

No. 35

35 DRAWLOOM SHAWL
1869–70
1.72 m × 1.22 m
Museum no. 617.972.2
Fabric Ground: silk twill. Fillover: wool
Fringe None
Manufacturer Towler, Rowling & Allen
Donor Mrs T Starling

Originally a full-sized shawl, this has been cut in half, possibly by two sisters on the death of their mother. The design on this half is facsimile to that on the prototype of the shawl given to Queen Victoria (no. 34).

36 DRAWLOOM SHAWL
1869–70
3.10 m × 1.67 m
Museum no. 182.976
Fabric Ground: silk twill. Fillover: silk and wool
Fringe Warp threads crimped
Manufacturer Towler, Rowling & Allen
Donor Miss D Whyte

A slightly different version of the shawl given to Queen Victoria on her visit to Norwich (see no. 34), or it is possible that this one is the prototype – who can tell? It seems unlikely as this one was bought in Scotland. Again it is possible that this could be a Scottish copy, as the design does not appear to have been registered at the PRO.

It is half blue and half red as to ground and has the same deep end borders as no. 34 and narrower side borders with a narrow flowery spray covering the meeting of red and blue.

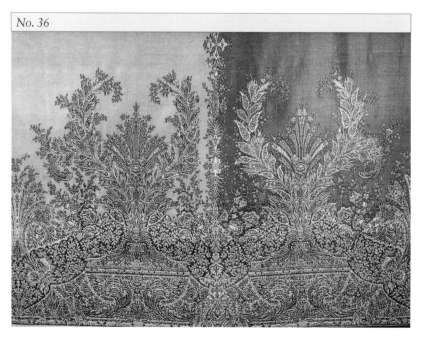

No. 36

Arab Shawls

From the middle of the 1840s until almost the demise of the shawl there was a fashion for a type called variously Arab (Norwich), Glasgow (Paisley) and burnous (costumiers and costume historians). This was semicircular, with the diameter at the top measuring some 3 m or so, and the radius of the arc about 1.5 m. There was often a tassel centre back. Generally, though not always, the fabric was of soft, clinging silk leno. They were often known in Norwich, though it is difficult to understand why, as 'Christening shawls'. Whether they were worn by the mother in the same way as the Paisley kirking shawls, or whether the baby was wrapped in them, is not known.

One particular firm in Norwich seems to have specialised in their manufacture, that of E & F Hinde. Luckily their order book for 1847–8 is in the Bridewell Museum in Norwich and, though to modern eyes it is partly incomprehensible, some significant figures appear. In the book the sales of thirty-three different types of shawls are recorded, among them five kinds of Arabs named as: Arab long, Arab all yarn, Low Arab,

Medium Arab and Super Arab. The shawl made for the managing director's wife (no. 38 in the Catalogue) must be a Super Arab, but as regards the categories into which the rest of those in the collection fit, one can only guess – possibly they are Medium Arabs.

From the designs and colouring it looks as if the firm had only one designer for these shawls. Most of the borders in particular are very similar with motifs in yellow on a ground of emerald green and scarlet alternately. These shawls are very thin and frail; most are disintegrating.

37 BLOCK PRINTED ARAB SHAWL
1845–50
3.5 m top edge (semicircular shawl)
Museum no. 160.984.4
Fabric Close silk leno
Fringe Silk knotted on semicircle
Manufacturer E & F Hinde
Donor Mrs Bates

This shawl has a design of small stubby pines packed closely over the ground in staggered rows in red, green and deep gold. The border is 15 cm deep with flowery shapes in alternate red and emerald green, divided by narrow purple stripes forming sections. There is a long tassel hanging from the centre of the straight top.

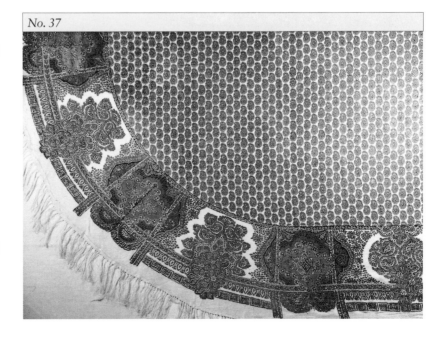
No. 37

No. 38A

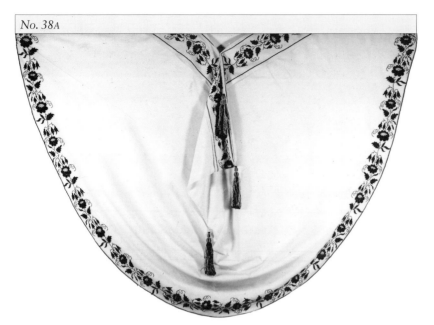

No. 38B

38 BLOCK PRINTED ARAB SHAWL
1850s
2.12 m top edge (semicircular shawl)
Museum no. 350.972.3
Fabric Very fine tabby weave, with silk warp and wool weft
Fringe None
Manufacturer E & F Hinde
Donor Mr S Hinde

This is an unique shawl in that it was specially made for the wife of the managing director of the firm of E & F Hinde, and as far as is known is the only one of its type. The fabric of white silk and wool is hand-embroidered round the border in a design of roses, bluebells and leaves in thick black silk. Instead of one, there are three tassels forming the hood centre back. They are made of black, white and fawn perlé silk.

39 BLOCK PRINTED ARAB SHAWL
*c.*1859
3.5 m top edge (semicircular shawl)
Museum no. 137.15
Fabric Silk warp and wool weft. Twill
Fringe Black heading with mauve and red silk strands. Sewn on
Manufacturer Probably E & F Hinde
Donor Miss Williams

The ground of this shawl has a different design either side of the centre back. One is of linked curving motifs and the other of motifs on red or green stripes. The border has alternate emerald and scarlet grounds for motifs mainly in deep yellow in a fern-like pattern.

No. 39

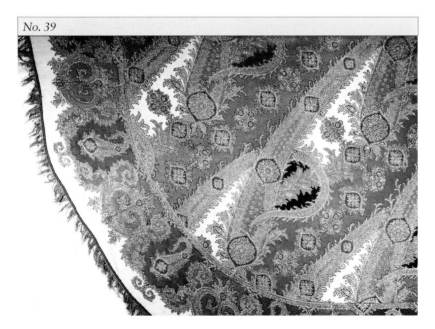

40 BLOCK PRINTED ARAB SHAWL
1860s
3.84 m top edge (semicircular shawl)
Museum no. 119.23
Fabric Close silk leno
Fringe Silk threads knotted on
Manufacturer Probably E & F Hinde
Donor Mrs G H Coe

The design of this shawl consists of all-over small motifs alternately full and half-size closely spaced to produce a trellis-like voided ground. The border, which is 10 cm deep all round, has large medallions with alternately a scarlet and a white ground and a beetroot arcaded edge and fringe. The main colours are dark green and plum with a little yellow. This shawl has never had a tassel.

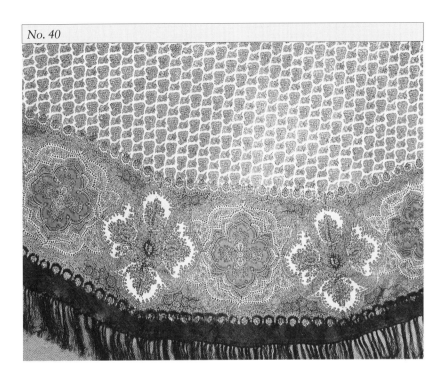

No. 40

41 BLOCK PRINTED ARAB SHAWL
1870s
3.24 m top edge (semicircular shawl)
Museum no. 306.966
Fabric Very soft silk leno
Fringe Twisted silk knotted on
Manufacturer Probably E & F Hinde
Donor Mrs Ratcliffe

This design is similar to others in the group. The ground has an all-over small formal motif with cream interstices forming a trellis, while the border has emerald green and scarlet bases for gold and black motifs. There are no pines. A silk tassel hangs from the centre of the straight edge.

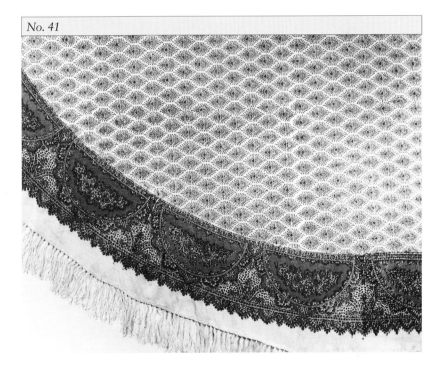

No. 41

42 BLOCK PRINTED ARAB SHAWL

1870s

3.20 m top edge (semicircular shawl)

Museum no. 275.970

Fabric Silk leno

Fringe Silk, knotted on

Manufacturer Probably E & F Hinde

Donor Anonymous

This shawl has a one-design all-over pattern consisting of small feathery diamond shapes, showing the cream ground as a lattice between. The semicircular border is of voided pines with some emerald green and letter-box red. The colours of the diamonds are mauve, black and gold.

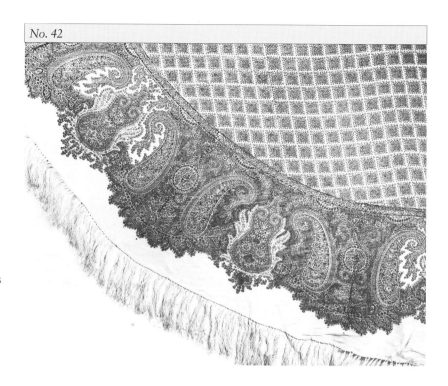
No. 42

43 BLOCK PRINTED ARAB SHAWL

*c.*1870s

3.24 m top edge (semicircular shawl)

Museum no. 134.956

Fabric Very fine silk leno

Fringe Tightly twisted silk knotted on

Manufacturer Probably E & F Hinde

Donor Mrs Elmhurst

The main part of the design of this shawl reverses mirror fashion centre back. It consists of long thin pines in a continuous pattern of leaves. The 24-cm-deep border is of scallops and garlands with naturalistic roses. The pines are mauve in old gold leaves, but the general effect is of reds and browns on cream. There is a very ornate 15-cm tassel with a button top on the straight edge centre back. The printing is superb.

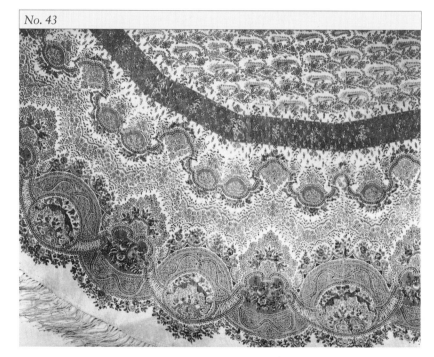
No. 43

No. 44

44   BLOCK PRINTED ARAB SHAWL
1870s
3.34 m top edge (semicircular shawl)
Museum no. 554.965
Fabric Silk leno
Fringe Short silk threads on heading. Sewn on
Manufacturer Probably E & F Hinde
Donor Mrs H Catton

Apart from the border there are two separate designs in this shawl, either side of the centre back: stripes of tiny geometric motifs, with bands of pine stripes alternating with 'plant in pot' motifs; very small closely packed pines.

The border is of medallions and tiny flowers with the medallions alternately emerald green and scarlet, as in so many of these shawls. The effect of the main design is of deep red on cream. There is no tassel. This shawl was originally purchased in 1875.

SHAWLS BY CLABBURN, SONS & CRISP

'Clabburn 1' Shawls

These are heavy, full size shawls, measuring, on average, 3.5 m by 1.5 m. The Museum owns nine such shawls and they all follow approximately the same style. They may or may not have a square or rectangular plain centre, not woven in twill as were most shawls, but in a plain, slightly ribbed weave. The end borders are deep, up to about 35 cm, and the side borders generally face into the centre. The majority were woven in the 1860s.

The art form Art Nouveau had its heyday in the 1890s. But in looking at some of these large shawls it becomes clear that by the middle of the 1860s the form had started. The long lines, lack of extraneous decoration and general reticence is there, and must have been a welcome change from the convolutions of the 1850s. By the 1860s two things were happening. First it was becoming clear that the era of the shawl was coming to an end, however slowly. The enormous crinolines had held the size and weight of the shawl in the 1850s, but now the fullness of the skirt was moving to the back with a straighter front to the dress. This trend continued until all fullness was draped at the back, which meant that a large shawl obscured the cut of the dress. Short jackets with a peplum to cover the bustle could be worn. The second thing which becomes clear is that invention

on the part of the designer was running out. All these shawls are designed to what is almost a formula. The same motifs are repeated again and again in different combinations and colourings. What is still superb is

the quality of the weaving and the amazing way in which very few colours could be made to give a totally different look to each shawl. They may have heralded the end of the shawl era but it was a lovely death.

No. 45

45 JACQUARD SHAWL
*c.*1861
3.47 m × 1.03 m
Museum no. 179.952
Fabric Silk
Fringe Fine warp threads, knotted in groups with two knots to each group
Manufacturer Clabburn, Sons & Crisp

Donor Lady Allison

This shawl is a facsimile design to no. 46 and appears to be a trial for the Paris Exposition of 1862. It is based on black with a black centre and, in the design, pale grey with touches of red, green and blue.

No. 46A

No. 46B

46 JACQUARD SHAWL
1862
3.47 m × 1.03 m
Museum no. 7.10.2
Fabric Silk
Fringe Fine wavy threads knotted in groups, with two knots to each group
Manufacturer Clabburn, Sons & Crisp
Donors Messrs F C Hinde and Walter Rudd

This is a superbly woven shawl, which gained a silver medal at the 1862 Exposition in Paris. It was initially awarded the gold medal but, owing to internal dissension, only the silver was given. It has a plain red centre and the design is a variation of the so-called 'scissor' pattern which appears so often at this time. Instead of pines the shape is more like a pair of curved scissors. The whole design is very fluid. John Funnell, who had designed for Towler & Campin, was the designer.

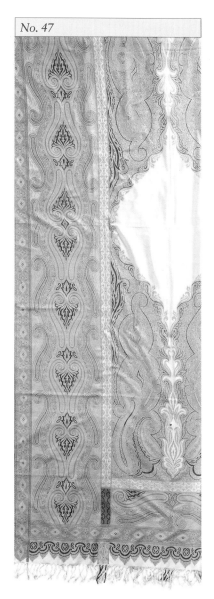

No. 47

No. 48

47 JACQUARD SHAWL
1863
3.10 m × 1.67 m
Museum no. 614.978.1
Fabric Silk
Fringe Warp threads mainly in
silver with a few in petunia or gold
Manufacturer Clabburn, Sons &
Crisp
Donor Bought

In 1863 Princess Alexandra of
Denmark married Edward, Prince
of Wales, and Norwich gave her
two shawls. This one is woven in

the Danish royal colours of red,
white and gold, and shawls 47, 48
and 49 in the collection appear to
be prototypes for the gift. Which
one was chosen is unknown. The
Norwich Mercury of 7 March
1863 was lyrical over its beauty
but omitted to describe it. Apart
from its colour and the fact that it
has no 'eye' in the centre, the
design of this shawl is identical to
no. 49. In one corner is sewn a
round medallion, the trade mark of
Clabburn, Sons & Crisp.

48 JACQUARD SHAWL
1863
3.55 m × 2.03 m
Museum no. 7.10
Fabric Silk
Fringe Fine silk warp threads,
single knotted in groups
Manufacturer Clabburn, Sons &
Crisp
Donors Messrs F C Hinde and
Walter Rudd

Another shawl in the Danish
colours of red, white and gold,
translated here into petunia, silver
and gold. Probably another
prototype for the shawl given to
Princess Alexandra in 1863. The
design is of large scrolls, sprays,
large and small pines arranged in
continuous wavy vertical stripes.
Very faded in part.

No. 49

No. 50

50 JACQUARD SHAWL
1863–6
3.65 m × 1.73 m
Museum no. 172.979
Fabric Silk
Fringe Warp threads, grouped into
a single knot
Manufacturer Clabburn, Sons &
Crisp
Donors Mr and Mrs Donald
Steward

This shawl is identical in design to
nos 51, 52 and 53, but has
different colouring – a black centre
with stripes in pale blue and light
green. The black has faded badly,
which gives the shawl a very
depressed look.

49 JACQUARD SHAWL
1863–70
3.10 m × 1.67 m
Museum no. 190.992
Fabric Silk
Fringe Warp threads knotted once
in groups
Manufacturer Clabburn, Sons &
Crisp
Donor Miss P Clabburn

Instead of a central rectangle, this
shawl has a long white motif
widening in the centre to enclose a
mainly crimson 'eye'. The
patterned field uses crimson, black
and yellow giving an overall bronze
look. Probably the prototype for
no. 47.

89

No. 51

51 JACQUARD SHAWL
1866
3.47 m × 1.03 m
Museum no. 40.937
Fabric Silk
Fringe Fine silk warp threads
grouped and knotted twice
Manufacturer Clabburn, Sons &
Crisp
Donor Bought

A shawl of identical design to nos.
50, 52 and 53, with a white centre
and stripes of strong blue and
emerald green. The long thin pines
and scrolls are in white, red and
black.

The shawl was given by the
retailer, N H Caley, Shawlman to
the Queen, as the first prize for a
Ladies' Archery Contest.

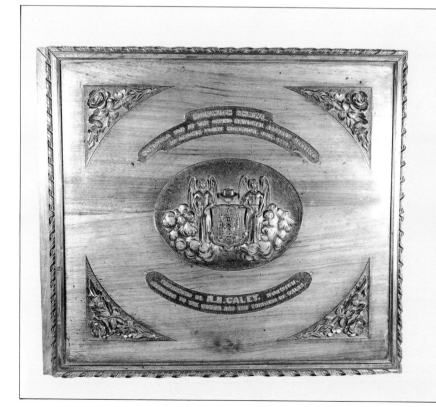

51A WALNUT BOX
56 cm x 50 cm x 6 cm
A box with a sliding lid carved
with a central boss carrying the
arms of the city of Norwich.
In each corner a cornucopia
containing the rose, thistle and
shamrock. The top legend reads:
'Norwich shawl competed for at
the Grand National Archery
Meeting at Crown Point
Norwich July 1866.' The lower
legend reads: 'Presented by
N H Caley Norwich Shawlman
to the Queen and the Princess
of Wales.'

52 JACQUARD SHAWL
1866
3.55 m × 1.64 m
Museum no. 8.969
Fabric Silk
Fringe Warp threads 9 cm long
with two knots holding each group
Manufacturer Clabburn, Sons &
Crisp
Donor Mrs Bracecamp

This is one of four identical designs
in different colourings (see nos 50,
51 and 53). The centre is a slightly
ribbed plain weave in crimson and
the deep border consists of long
thin pines and much interlaced
scrolling in vertical stripes. The
colours used – green, red, mauve,
blue and black – are more dotted
than solid, giving a changeable,
shot effect.

No. 52

53 JACQUARD SHAWL
c.1866
3.47 m × 1.47 m
Museum no. 113.946
Fabric Silk
Fringe Warp threads grouped into
a single knot
Manufacturer Clabburn, Sons &
Crisp
Donor Mrs Fitzmaurice

A plain cardinal red rectangular
centre has a deep border of long
thin pines and much interlaced
scrolling in vertical stripes of red,
dark green and ultramarine. These
colours, though strong, are
indefinite as other colours are
dotted, giving the same bronze
look as that of no. 49. See nos 50,
51 and 52.

No. 53

'Clabburn 2' Shawls

These are smaller than the Clabburn '1's, being approximately 2 metres square, on average. The Museum has a large holding of Clabburn '2's, and many are also privately owned in Norfolk. This is probably because they were among the last to be woven in the 1860s and 1870s and so had not the time to wear out before they became unfashionable. The Clabburn '2's were obviously more for hard wear whereas the Clabburn '1's were for social occasions.

The large majority of this group are woven in horizontal stripes which almost overlap with no background. The stripes are made up from motifs often taken from their smarter and larger sisters, the Clabburn '1's, and because of these stripes the shawls are known as 'Clabburn Zebras'.

No. 54

54 JACQUARD SHAWL
1850s
1.77 m × 1.68 m
Museum no. 1.930
Fabric Silk
Fringe Has been cut off below knot. Warp threads
Manufacturer Clabburn, Sons & Crisp
Donor Dr H Back

A shawl with an indefinite vertical stripe. A double serpentine outline has a double pine within each bulge, with smooth sprays waving over the outline, forming a wide stripe with a dropped design.

The warp is red with black and yellow and the shawl reverses to a wearable yellow and black with some red.

55   JACQUARD ZEBRA SHAWL
Late 1850s
1.72 m × 1.62 m
Museum no. 246.971
Fabric Silk
Fringe Warp threads
Manufacturer Clabburn, Sons &
Crisp
Donor Mr R A Clare

Horizontal stripes 4 cm wide, two
of which make up a unit,
composed of bands of flower
motifs, crosses, chevrons, etc. The
warp threads are crimson and the
colours are so intermingled that the
general effect is of a bronzy green.

This is one of the shawls which,
though not reversible, could have
been worn showing the back as the
front, in which case the colours
would be much stronger, dark
green and black with a little yellow
and white. Illustration shows both
right and wrong sides.

No. 55

56   JACQUARD ZEBRA SHAWL
1860s
3.55 m × 1.64 m
Museum no. 227.969
Fabric Silk
Fringe Missing
Manufacturer Clabburn, Sons &
Crisp
Donor Mrs Mawson

The horizontal stripe unit in this
shawl is 14 cm and is made up of
two patterns. They include circles
and serpentine motifs with almost
indistinguishable tiny pines
scattered through. The shawl is
very faded giving an attractive
pink/brown effect. Illustration
shows both right and wrong sides.

No. 56

57   JACQUARD SHAWL
1860s
1.75 m × 1.75 m
Museum no. 279.962.4
Fabric Silk
Fringe Warp threads knotted in
the stripe colours – red, blue and
red
Manufacturer Probably Clabburn,
Sons & Crisp
Donors The Misses Mann

An unusual shawl in that, while the
design is the same all through,
there are three equal stripes which
run up the shawl with mainly red
and black on the outside stripes
and blue and green on the middle
one. The design is of vertical
stripes of a vase of flowers
alternating with pines and
medallions with sprays between.

No. 57

93

58   JACQUARD ZEBRA SHAWL
1860s
1.60 m × 1.60 m
Museum no. 172.939
Fabric Silk warp with wool weft
Fringe Groups of warp threads knotted
Manufacturer Clabburn, Sons & Crisp
Donor Mrs F Shields

This shawl is very faded in parts giving a muted effect. The design is also indefinite and consists of horizontal stripes of varying widths with dense flowers, medallions, curving shapes and serpentine stems. The warp is of red stranded silk with black, green, blue and white.

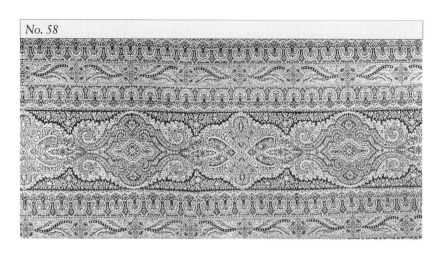

No. 58

No. 59

59   JACQUARD ZEBRA SHAWL
1860s
2.00 m × 2.00 m
Museum no. 263.987.2
Fabric Silk
Fringe Rather sparse warp threads
Manufacturer Clabburn, Sons & Crisp
Donor Doris Olive Gregory

Horizontal stripes of circular medallions alternate with black stripes which have upright stems of foliage growing into them giving a jagged effect to the black. The main colours are red and green, giving a general bronze effect. Illustration shows both right and wrong sides.

No. 60

60   JACQUARD SHAWL
1860s
1.70 m × 1.70 m
Museum no. 291.966.2
Fabric Silk
Fringe Stranded silk warp threads
Manufacturer Clabburn, Sons & Crisp
Donor Miss Pooley

The ground is covered with alternate vertical stripes, 10 cm wide with medallions and 5 cm wide with geometrical flowers. There is no strong colour, the effect being of a brownish red, with some black, blue and green.

No. 61

No. 62

61 JACQUARD SHAWL
1860s
2.00 m × 2.00 m
Museum no. 372.959
Fabric Silk
Fringe Sparse warp threads
Manufacturer Clabburn, Sons &
Crisp
Donor Miss J D Parkes

This shawl is identical in colour
and design to no. 67, woven by
James Churchyard. In fact there is
every reason to think that this one
may also have been woven by him
as most weavers kept to the same
design while it was still selling.

As with so many shawls of this
date and manufacture, the design
and colouring give an indefinite
effect. There are vertical stripes,
11 cm wide, of large circles, each
containing eight circular and one
central flower head. These alternate
with narrow geometrical flower
stripes. The warp is red stranded
silk and the colours merge to give a
red and green shot, indefinite
appearance.

62 JACQUARD SHAWL
1860s
1.78 m × 1.78 m
Museum no. 614.978.2
Fabric Silk
Fringe Warp threads with groups
slightly twisted but unknotted
except at ends of stripes
Manufacturer Clabburn, Sons &
Crisp
Donor Bought

A very striking shawl, obviously of
some importance but its weaver
and the purpose for which it was
made are unknown.

It has an all-over design with
four vertical stripes (5.5 cm). There
are many medallions, swirling
leaves and flower heads. The warp
is a deep petunia colour and there
is strong blue, strong green and
black, giving an iridescent look. At
one end is a round black printed
label with the legend 'Caley
Shawlman and Silk Mercer to the
Queen and Princess of Wales
Norwich. Importer of Continental
Manufactures' in gold lettering.
Illustration shows both right and
wrong sides.

63 JACQUARD ZEBRA SHAWL
1860s
1.78 m × 1.58 m
Museum no. 229.971.1
Fabric Silk
Fringe Warp threads grouped with
a single knot
Manufacturer Clabburn, Sons &
Crisp
Donor Mrs A N Orr

A very striking shawl in brilliant
colours. It has horizontal stripes
8.5 cm wide using the design which
is seen on borders in some of the
large shawls from the same firm.
These stripes are divided by 2-cm
stripes in strong emerald, crimson,
cobalt blue and black. The larger
stripes are in red, black and white.

No. 63

64 JACQUARD ZEBRA SHAWL
1860s
1.65 m × 1.60 m
Museum no. 962.968.4
Fabric All silk in two thicknesses
Fringe Warp knotted
Manufacturer Possibly Clabburn,
Sons & Crisp
Donor Miss T E Tuthill

This shawl is probably a Clabburn
Zebra but, except for the
horizontal stripes, there is no
definite clue. The stripes are
grouped in repeating units of
15 cm, of which 5 cm is of beige
medallions on green and 5 cm of
beige medallions on black. In
between are narrow stripes of tiny
motifs on red and white. The
thicknesses of silk used make for a
slightly bumpy effect.

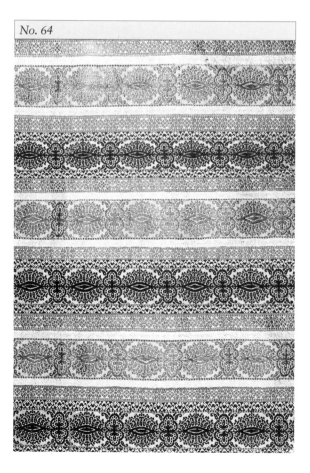

No. 64

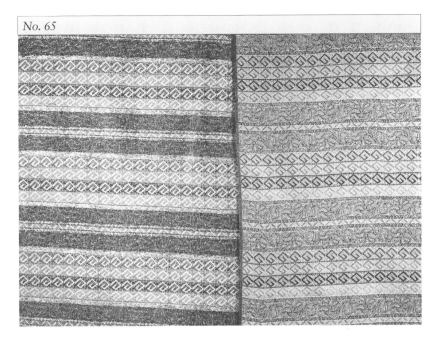

No. 65

65 JACQUARD ZEBRA SHAWL
1863
1.70 m × 1.60 m
Museum no. 279.962.2
Fabric Silk
Fringe Warp threads
Manufacturer Clabburn, Sons &
Crisp
Donors The Misses Mann

Stripes of four lines of a square-
angled pattern (no. 158226 PRO)
in mauve/blue, black, light petunia
and emerald, alternate with two
stripes of very smooth outlined
wavy leaves (no. 161796 PRO).
The warp fringe is crimson but this
colour scarcely appears in the
shawl. Illustration shows both right
and wrong sides.

No. 66

66 JACQUARD SHAWL
1865–75
1.70 m × 1.70 m
Museum no. 345.974
Fabric Silk warp, wool weft
Fringe Sparse warp ends
Manufacturer Clabburn, Sons &
Crisp
Donor Bought

A reversible shawl. The ground
design is of black and silver, with
strong diagonal lines and an
occasional small pine in foliage.
The ground is intersected by
occasional narrow (1-cm) stripes,
in light green, red and blue with
silver, which cut across the basic
fabric.

   This is a very late shawl and is
probably an upholstery fabric as
made by this firm with the stripes
added to make shawls. Other
shawls are known, in private
ownership, with the same ground
fabric but different coloured
stripes.

97

Shawls woven by James Churchyard

What little we know of his life is told at the end of chapter 8. We know that he worked for several different firms and that probably explains why the four shawls in the collection all woven by him (nos 67–70), are so unlike each other. At one time, possibly when working for Clabburn, Sons & Crisp, he made a number of hunting wrappers, or 'wroppers' as they were known locally. These were about 90 cm square, with a neat pattern generally incorporating the pine, and were worn by men, tucked inside their coats. One wrapper (not woven by James Churchyard as far as is known) was given to Edward, Prince of Wales on his visit to Norwich. Churchyard's great-niece has ten such wrappers and so the three wrappers shown (nos 71, 72 and 73) are put in with his shawls.

The shawls woven by Churchyard and catalogued here comprise: one from Clabburn, Sons & Crisp (no. 67) of which there is also a facsimile (no. 60) in the 'Clabburn 2' section, one of fine brocaded organza (no. 70), a printed one of thick wool (no. 69) and one with a very fine silk check pattern (no. 68). This more than anything shows the versatility of the Jacquard machine in the hands of a competent weaver.

No. 67

67 JACQUARD SHAWL
*c.*1860
1.77 m × 1.77 m
Museum no. 76.972.1
Fabric Silk
Fringe Warp threads knotted at selvedge
Manufacturer Clabburn, Sons & Crisp
Donor Bought from Mrs Rushmer, the weaver's niece

This shawl, woven by James Churchyard when he was employed by Clabburn, Sons & Crisp, is identical in colour and design to no. 60 and it seems likely that the latter was also woven by him. The design contains the well-known motif of a circle with eight circular flower heads and a central daisy head. Although there are several colours, the overall impression is of an indefinite plum. Illustration shows both right and wrong sides.

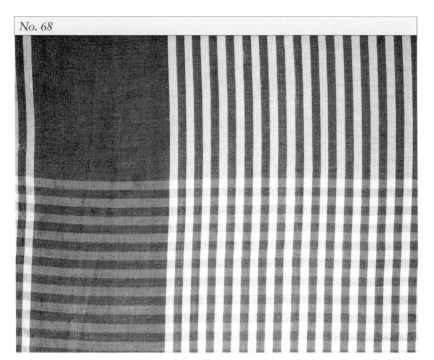

No. 68

68 JACQUARD SHAWL
1860–70
2.40 m × 1.62 m
Museum no. 76.972.2
Fabric Silk twill
Fringe Sparse silk knotted on at ends
Manufacturer Middleton, Answorth & Co. or Clabburn, Sons & Crisp
Donor Bought from Mrs Rushmer, the weaver's niece

A large shawl in 1-cm checks of tobacco brown, fawn and cream with a 13-cm band of brown 7.5 cm from each end and a corresponding band of fawn down each side.

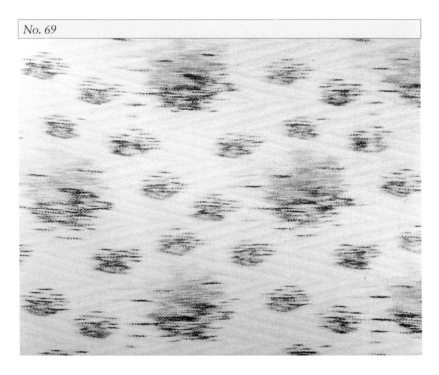

No. 69

69 PRINTED JACQUARD SHAWL
1860–70
1.44 m × 1.32 m
Museum no. 76.972.3
Fabric Warp-printed, warp-faced, multi-shaft point twill, wool
Fringe Warp threads heavily twisted at the ends, knotted into selvedges
Manufacturer Unknown
Donor Bought from Mrs Rushmer, the weaver's niece

The effect of this thick soft shawl is of chevron ridges in varying depths, with clouded red and brown splodges printed on cream wool.

70 JACQUARD SHAWL
*c.*1880s
1.52 m × 1.52 m
Museum no. 76.972.4
Fabric Fine silk organza
Fringe Thick wool knotted on all round
Manufacturer Unknown
Donor Bought from Mrs Rushmer, the weaver's niece

This is not technically a Norwich shawl, but shows one of the other types woven by different manufacturers. It consists of blocks of black, grey and cream organza brocaded at intervals with pink and silver naturalistic roses.

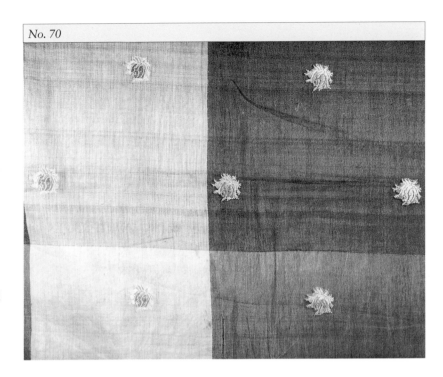

No. 70

71 JACQUARD WRAPPER
1860s
0.87 m × 0.87 m
Museum no. 361.972
Fabric Silk
Fringe None
Manufacturer Probably Clabburn, Sons & Crisp
Donor Mrs M Holmes

A man's wrapper with a most unusual design. There are pines, suns and other motifs on what resembles an inaccurate black and gold chessboard. The weaving technique used makes the colours glint.

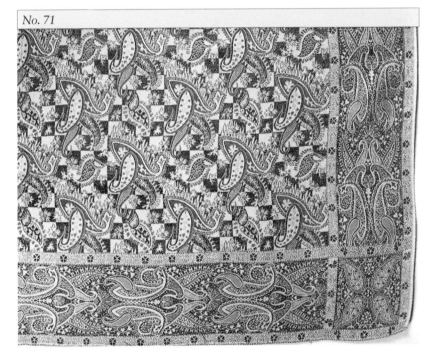

No. 71

No. 72 and 73 (right)

72 JACQUARD WRAPPER (*left*)
1860s
0.90 m × 0.86 m
Museum no. 168.967.7
Fabric Silk
Fringe None
Manufacturer Clabburn, Sons & Crisp
Donor Lady Gurney Collection

This wrapper has an identical design to no. 73 and illustrates the amazing difference that colour can make. The other wrapper is of a striking design in black and silver, while in this one the shot red, blue and green practically obliterate the design.

73 JACQUARD WRAPPER (*right*)
1860s
0.87 m × 0.87 m
Museum no. 183.977.4
Fabric Silk
Fringe None
Manufacturer Clabburn, Sons & Crisp
Donor Mrs M Downs

A man's wrapper which perhaps may count as a shawl. It has a striking design of silver swirling leaves and small motifs on a black ground, with a border of the horizontal heart-shaped motif seen on many of this firm's large shawls. An identical design to no. 72.

MISCELLANEOUS SHAWLS

74 HANDLOOM SHAWL
COUNTERPANE
1792
3.65 m × 3.65 m
Museum no. 41.95
Fabric Silk warp, wool weft
Fringe Silk threads from heading.
Sewn on
Manufacturer John Harvey &
P J Knights
Donor Unknown

No. 74

As this shawl counterpane came into the Museum when the latter was only one year old, the provenance is uncertain, but it is quite certain that it is the prototype for the shawl counterpane given to Queen Charlotte by P J Knights. It is the earliest piece of shawling that we know of. At this time, a distinction between shawls and shawling became pertinent. The latter is the fabric from which shawls were made, but the fabric was also used for counterpanes, hangings and even upholstery. The outline of the design was block printed on the fabric and then embroidered in a close darning stitch resembling weaving.

This counterpane has, in the centre, the Royal Coat of Arms with the French fleur-de-lys, Scottish lion, English leopards and Irish harp in the corners. The border has trailing sprays of roses and thistles joined with the Garter Star. Where the borders meet at the corners there is a crown surmounting 'G R'.

The counterpane is not in a good state of repair and it is hoped that the money may be found to conserve it.

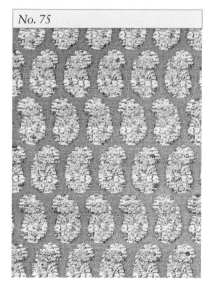

No. 75

75 DRAWLOOM SHAWL
*c.*1810
1.64 m × 1.64 m
Museum no. 183.977.2
Fabric Ground: silk warp, wool weft; twill. Fillover: wool
Fringe Rough warp threads at one end; the other end has been cut and machined at a later date
Manufacturer Said to be E & F Hinde
Donor Mrs M Downs

Identical to no. 75 but on a red ground.

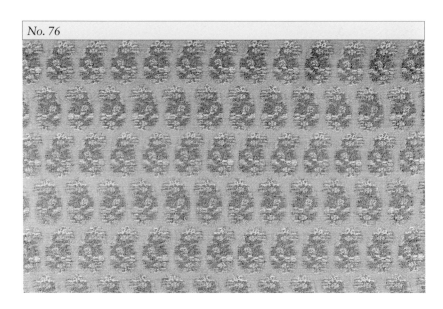

No. 76

76 DRAWLOOM SHAWL
*c.*1810
1.64 mm × 1.64 m
Museum no. 183.977.1
Fabric Ground: silk warp, wool
weft; twill. Fillover: wool
Fringe Rough warp ends at one
end; the other end has been cut and
machined at a later date
Manufacturer Said to be E & F
Hinde
Donor Mrs M Downs

This shawl and no. 76 are identical
except for the ground colour, in
this case either dark green or faded
black and in the other, red. The
design consists of small pines
dispersed alternately and closely
over the ground. Both shawls
appear to have been cut, or rather
torn, from yardage.

   These are the earliest shawls in
the collection and as such are early
drawloom. The donor said that
they were manufactured at E & F
Hinde, a firm which started in
1810 and became one of the
largest. Both shawls are crudely
though accurately woven and they
are very harsh to the touch.

No. 77

77 DRAWLOOM SHAWL
1810–20
2.56 m × 0.94 m
Museum no. 620.974.9
Fabric Ground: silk twill. Fillover:
wool
Fringe Sparse warp threads
Manufacturer Unknown
Donor Mrs Oakley

A long shawl or scarf which
resembles the Indian – it has a
plain deep petunia centre, with a
colour scheme of yellow, blue,
green and black. There is a deep
border of upright pines, slightly
turning over at the top with an
inner border of small upright pines.
The narrow outer-edge border is
woven in at the ends and sewn on
down the sides, which indicates
that narrow borders were being
woven by the manufacturer and
were not bought in.

78 DRAWLOOM SHAWL
1815
1.42 m × 1.42 m
Museum no. 133.22
Fabric Ground: silk twill. Fillover:
wool
Fringe Warp threads from long
lengths of ground fabric sewn on
all round
Manufacturer Unknown
Donor Miss F J Bayfield

This is one of the most delightful
shawls in the collection, largely
because of the very unusual old
gold colour of the ground. The
design consists of slips and sprigs
all over the fabric which is cut
from yardage. In design and colour,
the 2-cm sewn-on border bears
little relation to the ground, and
was probably made by a borderer.

The manufacturer has not been
identified, but it is known that
Elizabeth Bolingbroke bought this
shawl in Norwich prior to her
marriage to Samuel Woodward in
1815.

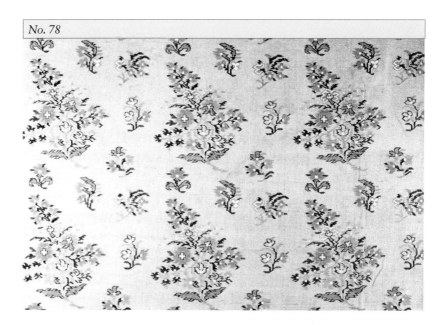

No. 78

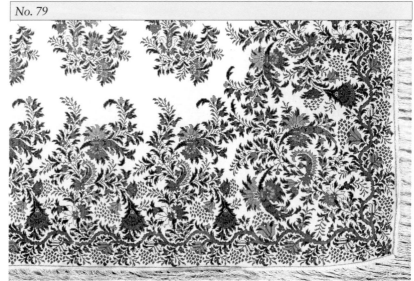

No. 79

79 DRAWLOOM SHAWL
1815–20
1.54 m × 1.54 m
Museum no. 293.974.2
Fabric Ground: silk twill. Fillover:
wool
Fringe Narrow heading with long
(15 cm) even fringe. Sewn on
Manufacturer Unknown
Donor Mrs Aldous

This shawl is a facsimile of no. 80,
except for the ground colour. This
one is on cream and the ground
consists of bunches of exotic
flowers and foliage in a mirrored
pattern. The border of the same
type of flower has a red serpentine
central stem. A red stem of this
type appears in other shawls and
could be a characteristic of one
designer.

No. 80

No. 81

80 DRAWLOOM SHAWL
1815–20
1.54 m × 1.54 m
Museum no. 617.972.1
Fabric Ground: silk twill. Fillover:
wool
Fringe Minute heading with 7-cm
silk fringe. Near-invisible stitching
for attachment
Manufacturer Unknown
Donor Mrs T Starling

This shawl is the twin to no. 79,
except that the ground and fringe
are plum colour.

81 DRAWLOOM SHAWL
*c.*1825
2.53 × 1.25 m
Museum no. 168.967.1
Fabric Ground: silk twill. Fillover:
wool
Fringe Sparse warp fringe
Manufacturer Unknown
Donor Lady Gurney Collection

A beautiful shawl which had been
made up as the lining of a silver
lamé opera cloak for use by Lady
Gurney, Lady Mayoress of
Norwich, at the Coronation of
George V in 1911. It is said that
she wore it over a dress specially
made of Norwich silk. As if with
great foresight, the shawl had not
been cut at all.

It has a deep pink ground and
has motifs (11 cm by 9 cm)
dispersed with smaller sprays
between. It is unusual in that,
although the two ends have the
same elements, the design is
different. There are large pines
38 cm high between narrow formal
bands.

105

82 DRAWLOOM SHAWL
1825–30
2.53 m × 0.80 m
Museum no. 173.979
Fabric Ground: silk warp, wool weft; twill. Fillover: wool
Fringe Sparse warp fringe
Manufacturer Probably Norwich
Donor Mrs Buchanan

Except for the ground colour, petunia instead of red, this shawl might well be Indian. The ground consists of horizontal and vertical rows of medium and small pines, facing in opposite directions, with swags of flowers between them. There is a narrow border which is nearly but not quite the same design as the narrow border which runs all round the shawl. The deep end borders have a row of upright pines. The colouring is of greens, blues and cream on petunia.

83 DRAWLOOM SHAWL
1827
2.79 m × 1.32 m
Museum no. 185.963
Fabric Ground: silk warp, wool weft; twill. Fillover: wool
Fringe The ends of the shawl are rolled and oversewn with warp threads as a short fringe
Manufacturer Unknown
Donor Bought

The ground of this shawl is covered with staggered rows of tiny red flowers with green leaves. The deep border has three rows of staggered pine shapes like bunches of flowers tied with ribbon. Sprays arching over the top of the pines. The colours are mainly red and green with some yellow, and a narrow blue edge border which divides the deep border from the ground. The name and date 'M R Dawson 1827' are embroidered on one side.

No. 82

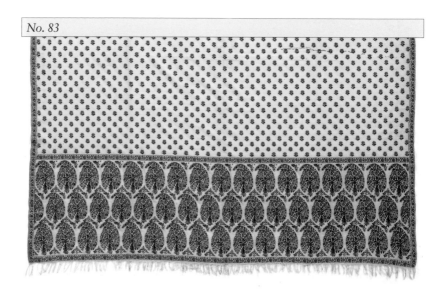

No. 83

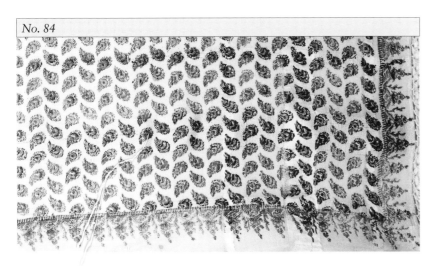

No. 84

No. 85

84 BLOCK PRINTED SHAWL
1820s
1.56 m × 1.53 m
Museum no. 94.939
Fabric Wool and silk leno quadrilled with silk twill
Fringe Long silk fringe knotted on
Manufacturer Probably Norwich
Donor Mrs Langton Barnard

The design includes a very neat arrangement of roses in small pine shapes in rows, alternately facing different ways; and a small neat border of upright motifs. There are few colours – only pink, red and green on a cream ground.

85 DRAWLOOM SHAWL
1820s
1.37 m × 1.37 m
Museum no. 285.964
Fabric Ground: silk twill. Fillover: wool
Fringe Silk from heading. Sewn on
Manufacturer Probably Norwich
Donors Mr and Mrs W P Cubitt

This shawl, though unobtrusive, shows early weaving at its best. The design is small and neat, with narrow floral stripes alternating with light wreathes. The colours are blue, red and old gold.

No. 86

86 DRAWLOOM SHAWL
Late 1820s
1.56 m × 1.56 m
Museum no. 17.943
Fabric Ground: silk twill. Fillover: wool
Fringe A sparse silk fringe hangs from a fabric heading
Manufacturer Unknown
Donor Miss Field

The cream ground is covered with sparse, angular, very diagonal motifs, giving a spotty effect with indefinite colouring. The border has a flower version of the Chinese Architectural style.

87 DRAWLOOM SHAWL
1825–30
1.60 m × 1.60 m
Museum no. 94.936
Fabric Ground: silk warp, wool weft; twill. Fillover: wool with some cotton
Fringe Warp threads
Manufacturer Unknown
Donor Dr C G Lamb

A shawl related to the Indian 'moon' shawl, but known in Norwich as a pot lid. These shawls in India always have a centre circle and four quarters in the four corners, but sometimes in Norwich the centre circle is missing. There are only two colours – red and blue on a cream ground – and the design is very densely geometric. This colour scheme appears on many shawls of the same date, especially the long kirking shawl.

88 DRAWLOOM SHAWL
Late 1820s
1.65 m × 1.65 m
Museum no. 729.966
Fabric Ground: silk warp, wool weft; twill. Fillover: wool
Fringe Twisted silk warp threads
Manufacturer Unknown
Donor Bought

A Norwich pot lid without the centre circle. The cream ground is covered with small pines in rows which face alternate ways. Each pine has in it a flower shaped, intentionally or unintentionally, like a St George's Cross. The four quarter-moons in the corners have dense flower patterns, and the outside border (5 cm wide) has a close design of palmettes and fronds. The colours are mainly red, yellow and light blue.

No. 87

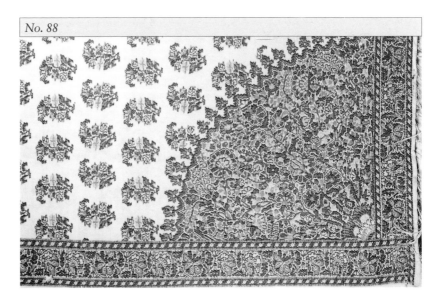

No. 88

No. 93

93 JACQUARD SHAWL
1830s
1.58 m × 1.58 m
Museum no. 24.980.1
Fabric Ground: silk warp, wool weft; twill. Fillover: wool
Fringe Long silk threads from a heading. Sewn on
Manufacturer Possibly Willett & Nephew
Donor Mrs Rainbird Clarke

This shawl has diagonal stripes of exotic flowers and foliage. The stripes are fairly solid with nothing between them, and they merge into the border with no division. The slightly uncertain weaving and the too-close cropping suggest that this is a very early Jacquard, made before the weavers had fully mastered the machine.

No. 94

94 JACQUARD SHAWL
1830s
1.64 m × 1.64 m
Museum no. 1004.968.1
Fabric Ground: silk warp, wool weft; twill. Fillover: wool
Fringe Warp threads
Manufacturer Possibly Norwich
Donor Miss D Symonds

From the look of the weaving this shawl could be an early Jacquard rather than a drawloom. The colours are hot – reds, yellow and green – and the design has sprays of exotic flowers and foliage joining all over the cream ground. The border is of tight flowers and foliage. In technique it bears a strong resemblance to no. 93.

No. 95

95 DRAWLOOM SHAWL
1830s
1.62 m × 1.48 m
Museum no. 2.976
Fabric Ground: silk; twill. Fillover: wool
Fringe Single strands of twisted silk (5 cm) sewn on to a narrow heading
Manufacturer Unknown
Donor Mrs J F Horth

A shawl with an outer border (10 cm) of exotic flowers and ribbons and an inner border of sprays of exotic flowers and foliage all round. There is one extra spray in each corner – this is a frequent feature of shawls made in the late 1820s and in the 1830s. The ground colour is cream and the general effect red with a little blue and green.

111

No. 96

96 DRAWLOOM SHAWL
1830s
1.52 m × 1.52 m
Museum no. 672.969.2
Fabric Ground: silk; twill. Fillover: wool
Fringe Silk knotted on to a narrow heading. Sewn on
Manufacturer Unknown
Donor Miss R Bateman

A superbly woven shawl with a well-cropped back. The ground has two exotic flower motifs in staggered stripes, forming a diaper effect. The border is of vases of exotic flowers and foliage alternately large and small. The colours are blue, green, red and yellow on a cream ground.

97 DRAWLOOM SHAWL
Late 1830s
1.82 m × 1.82 m
Museum no. 757.967.2
Fabric Silk warp and wool weft; twill
Fringe Warp and weft threads
Manufacturer Possibly William Stark
Donor Mrs Seaman

This shawl is of particular interest because it is woven of two different threads dyed approximately the same colour. Until about this time (the exact date is not known), shawls made from both silk and wool had to be cream as the dyers found it impossible to dye both threads an even colour. All coloured grounds were of silk only. On examination it is possible to see that even now the threads are not exactly the same colour, but they are near enough for use. The colour is the true Norwich Red invented by Michael Stark – it is more a pillar-box red than a crimson.

The owner of the shawl was the great-great-grandmother of the donor, and she married in 1840.

No. 97

No. 98

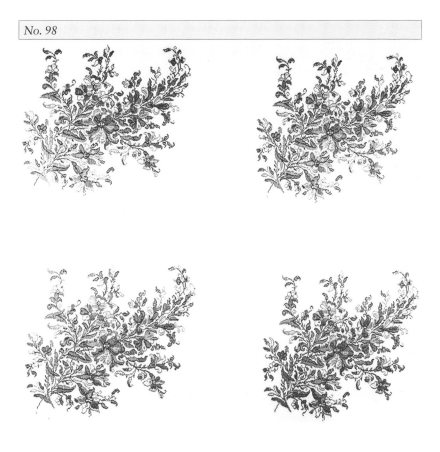

98 DRAWLOOM SHAWL
1840
1.55 m × 1.55 m
Museum no. 1994.66
Fabric Ground: silk warp, wool weft; twill. Fillover: wool
Fringe Sparse silk from heading grouped in one knot. Sewn on
Manufacturer Willett & Nephew
Donor Miss Wendy Hefford

This is a very important shawl for the collection as it is one of the very few which can be safely attributed to Willett & Nephew, one of the largest and most influential shawl manufacturers in the city. The design and colouring are typical of the date, with large isolated sprays round the edge and an extra one in each corner. Although the shawl has a very light effect there are six colours on cream: pink, red, blue, green, black and yellow.

No. 99

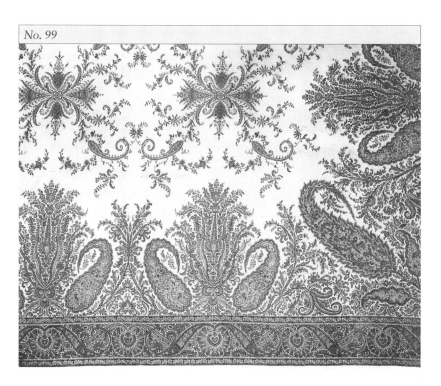

99 DRAWLOOM SHAWL
1840–5
1.73 m × 1.70 m
Museum no. 157.960
Fabric Ground: silk warp and wool weft; twill. Fillover: wool
Fringe Sparse silk warp threads
Manufacturer Unknown
Donor Mrs Blackett Swiny

A very hot-looking shawl with much red, yellow and green. In the design there is a lot of contrast between the solid outside border of massed large carnations and ribbon-like leaves and the much lighter inner border and centre.

The centre consists of nine large motifs with a four-flower centre, and from the corners long, thin, very curved pines and feathery swags emerge. The outside edge top and bottom is harlequin.

113

No. 100

100 DRAWLOOM BORDER
1842–5
1.45 m × 4 cm
Museum no. 146.946
Fabric Ground: silk warp, wool weft; twill. Fillover: wool
Fringe None
Manufacturer W Campling
Donor Anonymous

This piece of border is the only piece of weaving in the museum by W Campling. There are geometrical sprays of flowers and leaves (typical of this date), in red, green and yellow on dark blue. At some date the border was made into a bell pull, and it is of interest because of the woven label, 'W Campling', glued onto the back.

No. 101

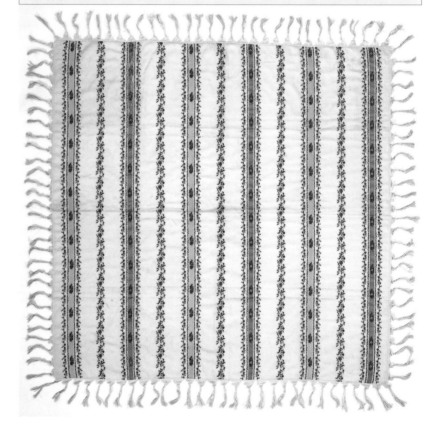

101 DRAWLOOM SHAWL
1842–5
1.57 m × 1.52 m
Museum no. 477.965.4
Fabric Ground: silk warp, wool weft; twill. Fillover: wool
Fringe Groups of silk threads 15 cm long with a single knot from a narrow heading. Sewn on
Manufacturer Unknown
Donor Mr R Restieaux

This shawl carries alternate stripes of orange and light blue on a cream ground. In the stripes are small isolated pine shapes every 12 cm. Each stripe is edged with tiny flowers. Between each stripe is an indefinite row of small flower sprays. On one corner is an indecipherable registration mark, which points to the shawl being later than 1842, the year when registration began.

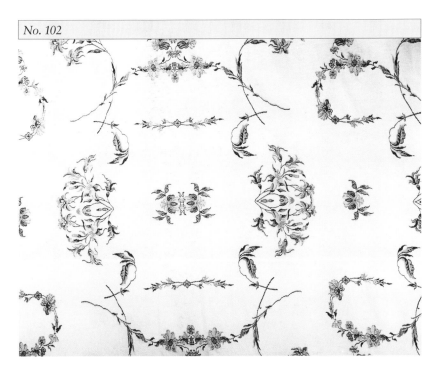

No. 102

102 DRAWLOOM SHAWL
1843
1.60 m × 1.60 m
Museum no. 225.956
Fabric Ground: silk warp, wool weft; twill. Fillover: wool and a little silk
Fringe Heavy silk knotted in groups. Sewn on
Manufacturer Unknown
Donor Mrs Bearman

The design of this shawl is light and elegant, with naturalistic flowers of reds and green on cream. The manufacturer is unknown, but pinned to the shawl was a note saying: 'This shawl was a present from my father. He had it expressly woven for me at Norwich about 1843.' Would that we knew where her father went to buy it.

No. 103

103 DRAWLOOM SHAWL
*c.*1840–5
1.40 m × 1.40 m
Museum no. 236.976
Fabric Ground: silk warp, wool weft; twill. Fillover: wool with a little silk
Fringe Heavy twisted silk on minute heading. Sewn on.
Manufacturer Unknown
Donor Miss D A Whyte

One of two shawls in the collection with a design of naturalistic flowers. A cream ground is covered with sparse sprays of pansies and fuchsias. It is a mirror design with pink, mauve and blue flowers on trailing criss-cross stems, with green and beige foliage and red stalks. The shawl was bought in the north of Scotland.

104 DRAWLOOM SHAWL
1843
1.70 m × 1.63 m
Museum no. 641.965
Fabric Ground: silk warp and wool weft; twill. Fillover: tabby weave in wool both single and double.
Fringe Black silk knotted on in groups
Manufacturer Probably Willett & Nephew
Donor Mrs O Haugh

An all-over design of exotic floral sprays in stripes, both vertical and horizontal, with small sprays between. The effect is of birds flying across the shawl. The general effect is creamy but is made up from small spots of different colours on a black ground.

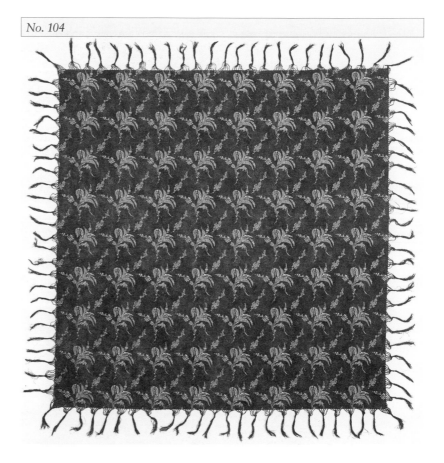

No. 104

105 DRAWLOOM SHAWL
1843
2.90 m × 1.50 m
Museum no. 620.974.10
Fabric Ground: silk warp, wool weft; twill. Fillover: wool
Fringe Sparse warp threads
Manufacturer Willett & Nephew (no. 9747 PRO)
Donor Mrs Oakley

This shawl has a design with long swirling pines merging into a plain red centre. There is a top border of small pines alternating with feathery pagoda shapes. The colours are blue, yellow, white and green on red.

No. 105

No. 106

106 DRAWLOOM SHAWL
1848
2.74 m × 1.52 m
Museum no. 3.968.1
Fabric Ground: silk warp, wool weft; twill
Fringe Black silk from heading, grouped into single knots
Manufacturer Unknown
Donor Miss Symonds

This shawl has a design which reaches nearly to the centre, leaving a small area of plain black. The design is of a dense pattern of randomly arranged pines and exotic flowers becoming lighter as they near the centre. The colouring is bright with blue, red, grass green, yellow and white.

It is known that the designer of this shawl was W S Morrison, but it is not known for whom he worked.

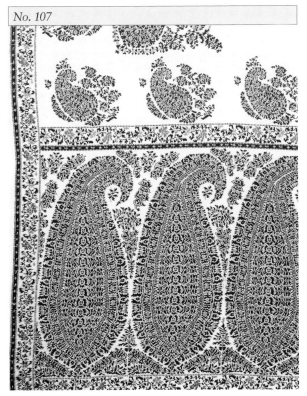

No. 107

107 DRAWLOOM LONG SHAWL
1840s
2.64 m × 1.32 m
Museum no. 458.961
Fabric Ground: silk warp, wool weft. Fillover: wool
Fringe Sparse silk fringe sewn on at the ends
Manufacturer Unknown
Donor Bought

This woven long shawl strongly resembles a Paisley pale-end or kirking shawl but it is considered to be of Norwich manufacture. It has a plain cream centre and a deep border of close large voided pines. The inner border is of isolated medium and small pines. In keeping with most shawls of this type, there are only three colours, two blues and a red.

117

108 DRAWLOOM SHAWL
1840s
1.60 m × 1.54 m
Museum no. 40.942.1
Fabric Ground: silk warp, wool
weft; twill. Fillover: wool
Fringe Long (12 cm) silk threads
on heading, knotted in groups.
Sewn on
Manufacturer Unknown
Donor Mrs Spurrell

This shawl is of a type which could
be from Paisley or Edinburgh but is
probably from Norwich. The
design is of trailing exotic flowers
coming from an urn-type motif at
the bottom of each stripe and
round the sides. The colours are
hot, mainly reds and yellows with
some green.

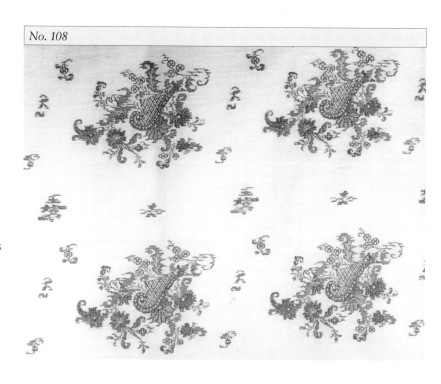

No. 108

109 DRAWLOOM SHAWL
1840s
3.40 m × 1.56 m
Museum no. 15.976.2
Fabric Ground: silk warp, wool
weft; twill. Fillover: wool
Fringe Warp threads
Manufacturer Unknown
Donor Mrs Chamberlain

Another shawl with an unusual
design. It has a plain black centre.
The deep border is tightly packed
with Persian-type flowers on which
there is imposed a voided pine
shape in black. These pines all turn
left. Above is an inner border of
smaller pines all turning right.
There are seven different colours
but the overall effect is of pink and
green.

No. 109

No. 110

No. 111

110 DRAWLOOM SHAWL
1840s
1.64 m × 1.54 m
Museum no. 493.973
Fabric Ground: silk warp, wool weft; twill. Fillover: wool with some silk.
Fringe Torn off
Manufacturer Unknown
Donor South Lopham Parochial Church Council, Norfolk

This shawl was found while being used as a table-cloth in a church vestry. The ground colour is brick red and the mirror design is of exotic flower sprays with a central sunburst. The border has fronds and flowers on a continuous stem. The colouring is very hot with an orangey brown, but is cooled by the addition of pale blue and white outlines.

111 BLOCK PRINTED SHAWL
1840s
1.50 m × 1.50 m
Museum no. 520.978.2
Fabric Plain tabby weave
Fringe None
Manufacturer Unknown but woven by George Harvey of Elm Hill, Norwich
Donor Mrs Madden

In the collection are two shawls woven by George Harvey, but it is not known whether he was a journeyman weaver or a manufacturer. The quality of the shawls is not up to saleable standard and it seems likely that he was a journeyman who may have made these for his family or friends.

The ground is white and the design comprises very long, curved diagonal pines, alternating with palm trees, bunches of flowers and leaves thrusting up from the edge as an indefinite border. The colours are very cool, being blue, green and pink.

119

112 DRAWLOOM SHAWL
1840s
1.52 m × 1.42 m
Museum no. 520.978.1
Fabric Silk warp, wool weft
Fringe Silk warp threads
Manufacturer Unknown
Donor Mrs Madden

This shawl of a most unusual colour for Norwich, but the weaver is known to be George Harvey of Elm Hill. The slight difference in the pink ground colour between the silk and the wool points to a date when William Stark was trying to dye the two yarns the same colour.

The design is typical of the time: horizontal rows of a thick trailing stem with exotic flowers and foliage in beige, yellow and a little blue alternate with rows of small isolated pines.

No. 112

113 DRAWLOOM SHAWL
1840s
1.54 m × 1.54 m
Museum no. 54.950
Fabric Ground: silk warp, wool weft; twill. Fillover: wool
Fringe Cream silk knotted on, mostly missing
Manufacturer Unknown
Donor Miss Mabel Holmes

This shawl has an unusual design. On the outside edge is a row of large pines, which have very heavy bases rising to a light question-mark shape at the top. There is an inside border of smaller, similar motifs with one extra motif in each corner. The colours are hot red and yellow on a cream ground, which gives the impression of flames. The shawl was woven by Samuel White of Magdalen Street.

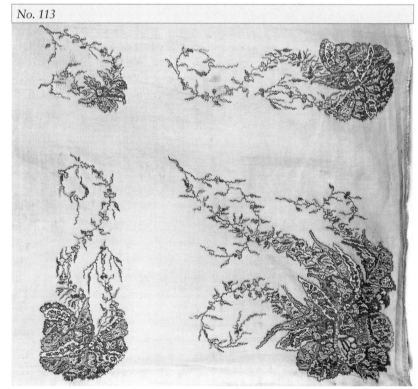

No. 113

No. 114

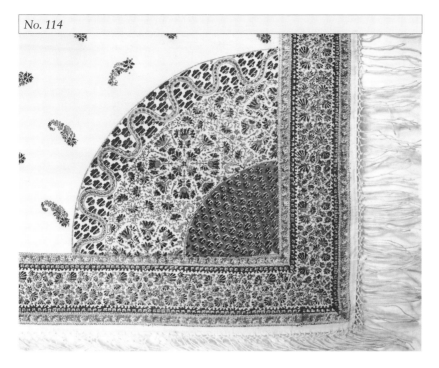

No. 115

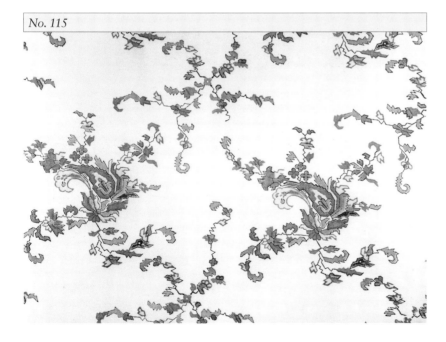

114   BLOCK PRINTED SHAWL
1840s
1.67 m × 1.67 m
Museum no. 619.972.1
Fabric Silk warp, wool weft; twill
Fringe Tightly twisted wool cross-knotted on
Manufacturer Probably E & F Hinde
Donor Miss J Roe

This shawl is of pot-lid design, with four quarter-circles in the corners but no central circle. The ground consists of isolated pines in diagonal rows with each pine at right angles to the next. The border is of tight sprays and the quarter-circles have isolated motifs and floral sprays. The colouring is rather spotty – royal blue, tangerine, grass green, cherry and pink on cream – but the inside of each quarter-circle is a strong red.

The donor's great-grandmother worked for E & F Hinde.

115   ROLLER PRINTED SHAWL
1840s
1.65 m × 1.65 m
Museum no. 677.971.1
Fabric Silk warp, wool weft; twill using very fine yarn
Fringe Fine silk on heading with groups joined in a single knot.

Sewn on
Manufacturer Unknown
Donor Miss R M Salt

This shawl is considered to be an example of early roller printing. It is noteworthy that, although in the collection there are no exact matches in design between woven and printed shawls, there is a strong resemblance between this one and no. 94.

The design consists of rows of small pines in a flowery spray. In the space between are light sprays. The design is very angular, in pink, red, green and black.

121

116 BLOCK PRINTED SHAWL
1852
1.52 m × 1.52
Museum no. 41.944.2
Fabric All wool
Fringe Hand twisted wool knotted
on
Manufacturer Unknown
Donor Mrs Yarham

This shawl has a plain cream centre, with long thin pines intruding into it. The border consists of swags of pendant flowers holding graceful pines, with many tiny flowers on stems giving a generally spotty effect. The colours are chiefly red and black and the printing is very sparse. This shawl, said to be Norwich, was worn by a bridesmaid to the donor's mother.

No. 116

117 BLOCK PRINTED SHAWL
1850s
1.15 m × 1.15 m
Museum no. 96.981
Fabric Wool twill
Fringe Single strands of wool knotted on at intervals
Manufacturer Probably Norwich
Donor Mrs P M Bowles

The cream ground of this shawl is covered with scattered flower sprays. The border has a bold design with pine-shaped flower clusters extending towards the centre, in blue and pink against a red ground. There are four narrow bands of flowers round the edge.

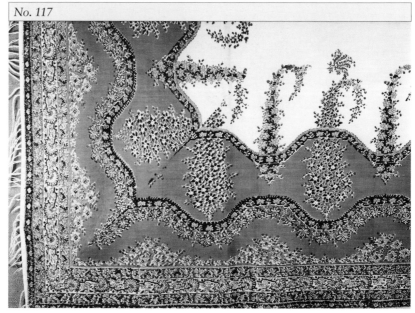

No. 117

No. 118

118 BLOCK PRINTED SHAWL
1850s
3.08 m × 1.57 m
Museum no. 27.953.1
Fabric Silk leno
Fringe Fine twisted silk, cross-knotted on heading
Manufacturer Possibly Norwich
Donor Miss A Robinson

The ground colour of this shawl is cream with a lot of rust, light blue and green and some maroon in the design, which consists of geometrical medallions filled with flowers.

No. 119

119 BLOCK PRINTED SHAWL
1850s
3.40 m × 1.78 m
Museum no. 253.981
Fabric Fine wool twill
Fringe Warp threads
Manufacturer Probably Norwich
Donor Mrs W Rackham

This shawl has a cream ground and a deep border of pine shapes, lozenges, feathery fronds and flowers. The border has geometrical outlines and, as well as the lozenges, it contains long hexagons and small squares. Inside the geometric shapes, contrast is provided by pines and flowers, the feathery tops of which face towards the plain centre of the shawl. The border colours are red and maroon, pink and pale green.

120 DRAWLOOM SHAWL

1850s

3.14 m × 1.54 m

Museum no. 16.24

Fabric Ground: silk warp, wool weft; twill. Fillover: wool

Fringe Warp threads

Manufacturer Unknown

Donor Mrs R Pym

This shawl has a plain black centre. The deep (65-cm) solid border is of interlaced scrolls and pines ending with a harlequin edge where each colour is sewn to the next, not woven together. The top of the border merging into the centre is feathery in pinks, blue and mauve.

No. 120

121 BLOCK PRINTED SHAWL

1850s

3.50 m × 1.45 m

Museum no. 1.979.1

Fabric Wool and silk leno. Thick silk leno stripes at intervals

Fringe Silk cross-knotted on heading. Sewn on

Manufacturer Unknown

Donor Mrs Broom

The printing of this shawl is so excellent that it may well have been done by the firm of Swaisland in Crayford, Kent, where a lot of high-quality printing was done for Norwich shawls. The colouring is quiet, mostly in reds and greens. The design consists of staggered rows of pines in various sizes all going in the same direction. There are 11 cm of scrolls, fronds, and at the edge a 6-cm strip of twisted band design.

No. 121

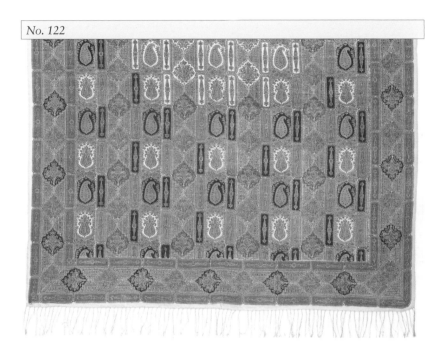

No. 122

122 BLOCK PRINTED SHAWL
1850s
3.45 m × 1.63 m
Museum no. 39.963.1
Fabric Closely woven silk gauze
Fringe Tightly twisted silk knotted on at 2-cm intervals
Manufacturer Probably E T Blakely
Donor The estate of Miss M L Page

This very precisely printed shawl is covered with motifs which vary from square to curved. They include pines, flowery batons and vases, and the colours, on a cream ground, are mostly reds and maroon with some green.

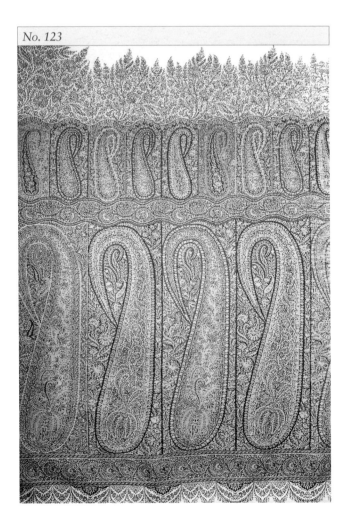

No. 123

123 DRAWLOOM SHAWL
1850s
3.14 m × 1.56 m
Museum no. 492.975
Fabric All-wool twill
Fringe Missing
Manufacturer Said to be E & F Hinde
Donor Mr E E Benest

A deep border with large pines voided alternately in light green, pale pink, reddish brown and dark blue. Above that another border with medium pines voided alternately in blue, pale orange and red. Above that, merging into a cream ground, are five spotty ferns. The shawl is in poor condition. It was said to have been bought at Chamberlain's, the retailers, and to have been woven by E & F Hinde.

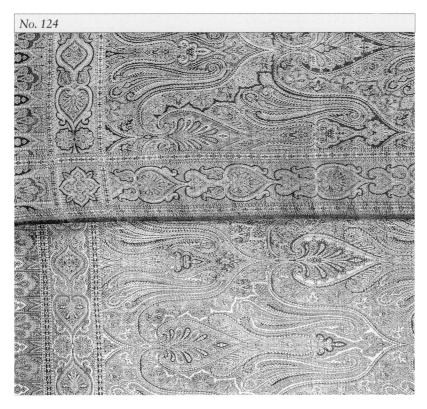

No. 124

124 JACQUARD SHAWL
*c.*1860
1.62 m × 1.62 m
Museum no. 12.964
Fabric Silk, reversible
Fringe Warp threads knotted
Manufacturer Unknown
Donor Professor J C Earl

This shawl, in two shades of purple with a little black and white, was probably made for half-mourning. The design is of narrow pines in arched shapes with a border of arcading. It can be worn reversed but it is not what is meant by a 'reversible shawl', which is always double-woven by one or another method.

The shawl is connected with Jessie Vincent, a weaver's granddaughter and niece to George Vincent, the Norwich School artist. Jessie married and lived in Lisbon with her husband Thomas Jones and they were the grandparents of the donor's wife. Illustration shows both right and wrong sides.

No. 125

125 JACQUARD SHAWL
1860s
1.70 m × 1.70 m
Museum no. 64.983
Fabric Double cloth in tabby weave. Wool warp and weft
Fringe Warp edges turned over and hemmed down and warp threads knotted on as fringe
Manufacturer Probably C & F Bolingbroke & Jones
Donor Mrs W West

A reversible shawl in hot colours of red, orange-brown, yellow, white and black. The design consists of a large repeat of formal flower sprays enclosed in scrolls and serpentine shapes. The knotted fringe is in the colours of the design.

No. 126

No. 127

126 JACQUARD REVERSIBLE SHAWL
1860s
1.77 m × 1.77 m
Museum no. 611.962
Fabric Double-faced cloth with silk warp and linen weft
Fringe Silk in the warp colours of white, yellow, red, green and black, knotted on
Manufacturer Probably C & F Bolingbroke & Jones
Donor Miss G Ball

A double-faced reversible shawl, similar to that woven by William Armes (no. 127), so probably from the firm of C & F Bolingbroke & Jones. The design is of large scrolls, almost snail-like, all over the ground. The end border is of long semicircular partitions each filled with a shell-shaped motif. The ends are turned over and sewn and the selvedges are woven separately and sewn on. The colours are red, cream and dull green, with no ground colour.

127 JACQUARD REVERSIBLE SHAWL
*c.*1860
1.78 m × 1.78 m
Museum no. 763.967
Fabric Double cloth woven in wool with the wool used both single and double
Fringe Traces of warp threads knotted onto binding
Manufacturer Probably C & F Bolingbroke & Jones
Donor Miss H A Baker

A Jacquard reversible shawl. William Armes the great-grandfather of the donor, wove it and family tradition held that though he worked from home he took his weaving back to St Clement's Alley. At that date the only manufacturer there was C & F Bolingbroke & Jones.

The design is of all-over scrolled pines and sprays in two different colour schemes mirrored in horizontal stripes of red and green. The swirling design foreshadows the Art Nouveau style.

127

128 JACQUARD SHAWL
1860s
3.44 m × 1.74 m
Museum no. 347.984.15
Fabric Silk
Fringe Removed
Manufacturer Probably Clabburn,
Sons & Crisp
Donor Mrs Stockings

This shawl has been adapted to
serve as a bedspread, one of the
more suitable uses for a full-sized
shawl. It is horizontally striped
with plain black alternating with
stripes of pines like flowers open or
shut with shaped edges in red and
yellow.

No. 128

129 JACQUARD SHAWL
1860s
3.14 m × 1.60 m
Museum no. 92.946
Fabric Ground: Silk warp, wool
weft; twill. Fillover: silk
Fringe Sparse warp threads
Manufacturer Unknown
Donor Miss Rachel Stocks

This is the only shawl in the
collection to have a silk instead of
a wool fillover. It seems possible
that it came originally from Messrs
Stark, the dyers, who either did
some weaving themselves or worked
closely with a weaving firm. The
centre is of Norwich Red, which by
this date was out of fashion,
crimson having taken its place.

The shawl has very deep borders
of attenuated pines with curved
bases filled with circles, stars and
other motifs. Narrower borders at
the sides have short pines with
onion-dome motifs. There are only
three colours: gold and green on
Norwich Red.

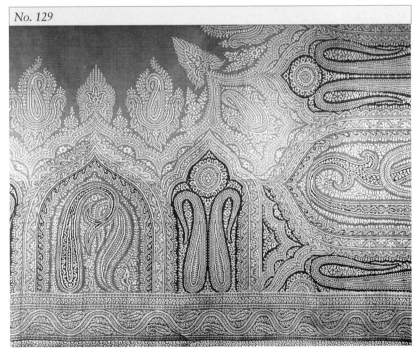

No. 129

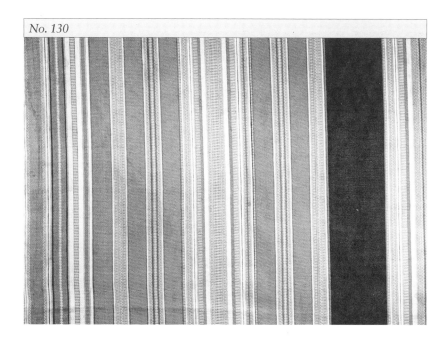

No. 130

130   JACQUARD SHAWL
Late 1860s
1.67 m × 1.67 m
Museum no. 477.965.1
Fabric Horizontally ribbed silk
Fringe Heavy silk twisted on
heading. Sewn on
Manufacturer C & F Bolingbroke
& Jones
Donor Mr R Restieaux

The only shawl in the collection to
sport the fashionable Roman
stripes. It is probably no
coincidence that this firm also
wove puggarees, as the style is very
similar here. There are five black
stripes in the centre and one in blue
at each edge. In between are less
intensive stripes in red and yellow.
The fringe is in the same colours.

No. 131

131   BLOCK PRINTED SHAWL
*c.*1870
1.52 m × 1.52 m
Museum no. 295.971
Fabric All wool; twill
Fringe Light silk with single knot
in groups
Manufacturer Unknown
Donor Mrs H Jarrold

The design shows a ground of
exotic flowers and trailing stems
with much hatching. There is a
deep border of pines in geometrical
shapes. The colours include equal
amounts of red and blue with
green and yellow.

The shawl was worn at the
donor's wedding by her
grandmother.

129

132 BLOCK PRINTED SHAWL
*c.*1880
3.50 m × 1.62 m
Museum no. 551.965
Fabric Silk warp, wool weft; twill
Fringe Maroon knitting wool, knotted on
Manufacturer Probably John Sultzer
Donor Mr R Woods

This shawl has two wide horizontal stripes repeated on alternate grounds of green and brown. There is a completely distinct design in each stripe. One has large voided pines of an odd shape with dense flowers. The other is covered with ten rows of closely packed small pines facing alternate ways.

This shawl was used for the christening of the donor, whose mother worked for John Sultzer.

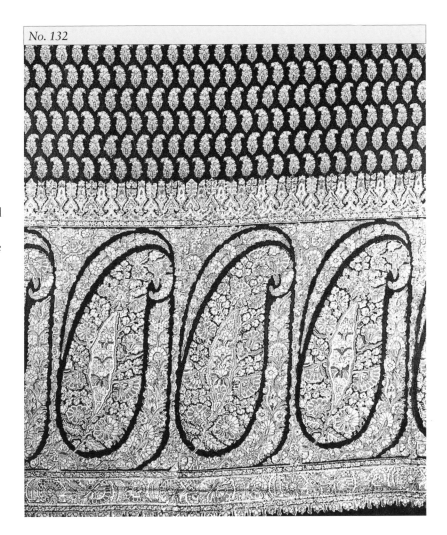

No. 132

133 BLOCK PRINTED SHAWL
*c.*1880
3.29 m × 1.75 m
Museum no. 10.969
Fabric Silk warp, wool weft; twill
Fringe Black knitting wool, crimped and knotted on
Manufacturer John Sultzer
Donor Miss Barnard

This shawl has a ground of indefinite stripes, one of rose medallions, the other of lozenge medallions. The border is flowing with flowerets, medallions and clustered droplets. The colours are mostly reds on cream with a maroon border.

No. 133

No. 134

134   JACQUARD SQUARE
*c.*1860
0.41 m × 0.41 m
Museum no. 120.14
Fabric Silk
Fringe None
Manufacturer Willett & Nephew
Donor Mr C J A Howes

This is in no way a shawl but eight pieces of shawl fabric sewn together to make a square, which may well have been intended as a cushion cover. The value of the piece to the collection is that it is the only fabric known to have been designed by Obadiah Short (1803–1886) and woven by Willett & Nephew for whom he worked. Obadiah was also a minor member of the Norwich Society of Artists. The design shows a long pine and lily shape mirrored in each quarter.

Appendix: Norwich Manufacturers

This chapter provides the names, addresses and any known details of the shawl manufacturers of Norwich. There is no such list in existence and much information has been lost over the years. What is here has been gleaned from street and commercial directories (which were published at irregular intervals), census returns, the newspapers and various articles and books on the city of Norwich. Unfortunately all these sources do not agree, which has resulted in some confusion over dates etc., but it seemed that a slightly inaccurate list would be better than none, and would provide a platform from which later researches could start. A few retailers, who had a great interest in shawl production, have also been included. Unless otherwise stated, all addresses given are in Norwich.

J H ALLEN & CO.
Shawl and dress fabric manufacturer
Elm Hill and St James Factory, also London and Manchester
First noted 1877
Last noted 1889
Said to have made the shawl worn by Queen Alexandra at her wedding.

WILLIAM ATKINS
Shawl manufacturer
28 Lower Westwick Street
First noted 1801
Last noted 1807
1803 Signatory as Master Weaver to the Wages Agreement.
1807 Patented improvement in the construction of a loom for weaving borders or stripes on different colours of shawls, or cotton, linen, silk or worsted goods (pat. no. 3054).

ROGER BAKER
Shawl manufacturer
Peacock Street
Noted 1810

WILLIAM BARCLAY
Shawl and bombazine manufacturer
5 White Lion Street
Noted 1801

JOHN BARLOW
Shawl manufacturer
St Margaret's Churchyard
First noted 1803
1803 Signatory as Master Weaver to the Wages Agreement.

JOHN BARLOW
Shawl manufacturer
Upper Westwick Street
Noted 1810

JOHN BARLOW
Shawl manufacturer
Middle Westwick Street
1836 Richard Jeremiah Barlow, shawl manufacturer, St Margarets Street.

EDWARD BARROW
Shawl and cotton manufacturer
20 Colegate
First noted 1783
Last noted 1813
Born in Manchester 1744
1783 Yarn factor in Norwich.
1784–5 '. . . succeeded in making a figured scarf in imitation of the Indian shawl, but it was too dear to find a sale and the manufacture was discontinued' (Mrs Barwell, *A Companion to the Norwich Polytechnic Exhibition*, Norwich, 1840).
1788 Sale of stock-in-trade of Edward & Isaac Barrow, including 8 dozen Norwich shawls.
1813 Died in St Saviours Parish.

CHARLES BASEY
Shawl manufacturer
Noted 1810

JAS. G J BATEMAN
Silk dress and shawl manufacturer
Gildengate
Noted 1846

A BELOE
St John Timberhill
Noted 1825
1825 Account of the employed weavers' riots: 'After this they proceeded to Mr A Beloe's factory in S John Timberhill where, Mr Beloe being in London, they immediately broke all the windows of this extensive factory which is four stories high' (*Norwich Mercury*, 4 February).

JAMES BLAKE
Shawl manufacturer
First noted 1803
Last noted 1810
1803 Signatory to Wages Agreement as Master Weaver.

ROBERT BLAKE
Cotton (1801); bombazine, crêpe and shawl (1822) manufacturer
Heigham Street

EDWARD BLAKELY
Shawl and silk manufacturer
75 London Street (formerly called Cockey Lane); 7 Conduit Street and Regent Street, London
First noted 1824
Last noted 1889
1831 *Norwich Mercury*, 5 March: 'Her Most Gracious Majesty the Queen and HRH the Duke of Sussex having condescended to patronise the manufacturer of Norwich shawls, Edward Blakely begs most respectfully to inform the Nobility and Ladies that he will have ready for inspection on

Tuesday 15th inst. a splendid assortment of the same description of Shawls which Her Majesty has been pleased to select . . .'

1848 Wm Piper, an employee of Blakely, suggested that 'as an antidote to the spread of revolutionary ideas among working men' he should 'advocate the encouragement of home interests among the upper classes'. Piper went to London, 'obtained an introduction from the Countess Spencer to the Queen and was able to effect sales of Norwich shawls with Her Majesty, the Queen Dowager, the Duchess of Kent and many members of the aristocracy.' (From the *Star of the East*, 16 April 1889).

1849 Received the Large Silver Medal of the Society of Arts for his shawl fabrics.

1849 Advertised that he had manufactured and printed some shawls entirely of Norfolk wool, 'the growth of John Hudson Esq. of Castle Acre' (*Norwich Mercury* 4 August).

1850 Competition of the Society for the Encouragement of the Arts, Manufacturers and Commerce, entry no. 98: 'Specimen of shawl weaving, being the first attempt to produce an increased effect by the introduction of gold thread in the shuttle' (competition catalogue).

1850 Advertises 'silk grenadine shawls, printed in natural flowers'. Address given: 15–16 London Street; manufactory and print works at the River House, Dukes Palace, Norwich (*Norfolk Chronicle*, 15 June).

1851 Showed at the Great Exhibition: cashmere green scarf with gold introduced; shawls of cashmere wool designed by John Funnell; Anglo-Indian scarfs, shawls, dresses, brocades etc. Received two orders for 'their beautiful shawls made in the pure Indian style' from Her Majesty.

1856 'E Blakely, Queen Street, Norwich. Silk Mercer, Shawlman and Furrier to Her late Majesty, the Queen Dowager. Funerals completely furnished' (billhead in private collection) Probable shawl: cat. no. 122.

EDWARD T BLAKELY

Manufacturer and retailer of silks, shawls, scarfs, mantelet, etc. Funeral furnisher
15 Cockey Lane

First noted 1820
Last noted 1824
Probable shawl: cat. no. 92.

JOB BLYTHE

Shawl manufacturer
St Pauls

1797 Given £25 from the Thomas Doughty Fund as a loan for setting up business.

1808 The Mayors' Court 'Ordered that Job Blythe of St Pauls, Shawl Weaver, have Sir Thomas White's donation No. 35 . . .' (£25).

BOLINGBROKE, ENFIELD & CO.

Shawl manufacturer
St Clements
First noted 1830
Last noted 1842

C & F BOLINGBROKE & JONES

Manufacturer of fancy goods and dress fabrics, especially poplins and shawls
St Clements, Calvert Street and St James Factory
First noted 1857
Last noted 1889

1862 International Exhibition. Exhibited shawls as well as many dress fabrics.
Have steam-power mills in Calvert Street and occupy a steam-power shed at St James Factory (no date).
Known shawls: cat. nos 127 and 128.
Probable shawls: cat. nos 125 and 126.

PHILIP BREEZE

Shawl manufacturer
Press Building
First noted 1830
1851 Census: shawl manufacturer.

BREEZE & COCKADAY

Fringe manufacturer
St Andrews Hill
Noted 1846

WILLIAM BROWN

Shawl manufacturer
St Clements
First noted 1830
1851 Census: aged 69. Living in St Helen's Hospital.

PETER BROWNE

Shawl manufacturer
St Marys
Noted 1822

CALEY BROS

Mercers, drapers, lacemen and furriers (retailer)
15 London Street
First noted 1857
1862 'N H Caley, Shawlman by especial appointment to Her Majesty the Queen' (catalogue of the International Exhibition, London).

JOHN CAMPLING

Shawl manufacturer
St Benedicts (1830) and Cowgate Street (1836)

WILLIAM CAMPLING

Shawl maker
Barrack Street and Pitt Street (1845)
First noted 1842
Last noted 1845
Attributed shawl: shawl border, cat. no. 100.

THOMAS CLABBURN

Shawl manufacturer
Magdalen Street and Pitt Street
First noted 1830
1851 Census: aged 62. Manufacturer of shawls and dresses, employing 500 men, at 36 Pitt Street.

CLABBURN & PLUMMER

Manufacturer of dress fabrics and shawls
Pitt Street
First noted 1844
Last noted 1850
1844–9 Registered twenty-nine designs for woven shawls and nine designs for printed shawls at the PRO.

CLABBURN, SONS & CRISP

Manufacturer of dress fabrics and shawls
Pitt Street
First noted 1851
Last noted 1883
1851 HRH Prince Albert 'purchased one of their justly admired and richly executed Hunting Wrappers'.
1851 At the Great Exhibition showed figured cashmere shawls, spun silk, fancy silk and Albanian silk shawls. W H Clabburn was a Juror for Class 15. The Queen bought a cashmere and silk shawl.
1852–72 Registered eighteen designs for shawls at the PRO.
1855 At the Paris Exposition gained a first-class medal for a reversible shawl.

1862 At the International Exhibition, London, received a medal for silk shawls of superior quality and design.

1863 Made three shawls for presentation to Princess Alexandra of Denmark on her marriage to Edward, Prince of Wales.

Known shawls: cat. nos 45–56, 58–63, 65–67, 71–72. Probable shawls: 57, 73 and 130. Possible shawls: 64, 68.

COOKE & CO.
Shawl manufacturer
Gildengate
Noted 1810

CUNDALL & KERR
Shawl manufacturer
The Walk
Noted 1863

JOHN DINGLE JNR
Shawl manufacturer
38 Botolph Street
Noted 1801

WILLIAM EASTWOOD
Shawl manufacturer and draper
21 White Lion Street
1825 Advertisement: 'sells elegant silk shawls – Turnover Handkerchiefs, Shawl Borders and Scarf ends. Shawls new bordered, Fringed and cleaned to look equal to new' (*Norwich Mercury*, 15 July).
1827 Announced in an advertisement that he was leaving Norwich for London and was selling off at half-price 2,000 silk shawls from 6s. 6d. to £3 13s. 6d. and 10,000 sets of shawl borders and fringes (*Norwich Mercury*, 27 January).

PHILIP BUXTON ETHERIDGE
Shawl maker
St Swithins
First noted 1822
Last noted 1857
1826 Bankrupt (*Norwich Mercury*, 12 January).
1839 'Mr Etheridge complains much of the piracies of Scottish manufacturers' (*A Commission to Report on the Conditions of the Hand-loom Weavers*, 1839, p 388).
1842 St Martins at Palace
1857 Census: aged 65, retired.

JOHN FISH
Shawl and cotton manufacturer
Fishgate Street
First noted 1801
Last noted 1811

JOHN FRANCIS
Shawl and dress fabric manufacturer
Calvert Street
First noted 1809
Last noted 1851
1809 Received a loan of £25 from Thomas Doughty Fund.
1823 Patented 'an improvement in manufacture of a certain fabric composed of silk and worsted to useful purpose' (pat. no. 4776).
1845 'A manufacturer of bandannas, shawls etc. Employs 180 persons (107 female). Women weavers earn 6/- weekly' (*Norfolk Chronicle*, 25 January).

THOMAS FRANCIS
Bombazine, crêpe and shawl manufacturer
St James
Noted 1822

GEARY & SULTZER
Shawl, stocking, and glove manufacturer
St Augustines
Noted 1845
Had 600 workers and a school connected with the factory (no date).
Registered one woven shawl design at the PRO (no date).
1863 Geary is listed as a manufacturer.
See also John Sultzer

GEARY, SULTZER & GEARY
Cheese factor
Noted 1823

H H GIBBS
Shawl manufacturer and importer of Irish tabinets
8 Market Place
First noted 1811
Last noted 1822

JOSHUA GOOCH
Fringe manufacturer
Duke Street
Noted 1846

JEREMIAH GRAVES & SON
Manufacturers of bombazines, crêpes, shawls, scarves and stuffs
St Georges
Noted 1822

GROUT & CO.
GROUT, BAYLES & CO.
GROUT, RINGER, MARTIN & CO.
Silk manufacturers
Pattesons Yard, Magdalen Street (1807) and New Mills, Lower Westwick Street (1815)
First noted 1807
Last noted 1894
Also had works at Ponders End, Great Yarmouth, North Walsham, Saffron Walden, Bocking, Mildenhall and Bungay; and a warehouse at 46 Gutter Lane, London
These firms worked entirely in silk, especially Canton silk. Their speciality was crêpe, and until 1827 they made few shawls. Information from the firm's accounts:
1825–1834 Printing in Norwich.
1831 Shawl manufacture increased and London warehouse moved from Gutter Lane to Goldsmith Street.
1832 London warehouse had moved to Foster Lane and Gutter Lane was taken over by Courtaulds.
1832 Dyeing and finishing at Ponders End.
1834 Had 1 London Jacquard and 4 Scotch Jacquards in Great Yarmouth and 148 power looms in Bungay.
1894 Became a Joint Stock Company.

THOMAS GUNTON
HENRY GUNTON
Manufacturers of shawls and hair cloth and curled hair for seating
Pitt Street (1836), Gildengate (1842), 182 Princes Street (1851), Elm Hill (1852) and St Miles (1869)
First noted 1836
Last noted 1869

JOHN HARVEY
Shawl and fabric manufacturer
St Clements
First noted 1788
1788 In a letter to Mr More, Secretary of the Society of Arts, Alderman John Harvey states: 'In a manufactory of shawls which I have invented, my

constant endeavour has been to procure wool sufficiently soft . . .' (*Transactions of the Society of Arts*, vol. VII).

1789 'Mr Harvey has engaged to weave a shawl 1½ yards square, all of wool of 180 skeins to 1lb. to be doubled and twisted for the warp; and the same single, or finer, for the woof [weft].' (*ibid.*).

1790 Duke of Norfolk inspects the factory of Messrs Harvey & Sons. (*Norwich Mercury*, 21 October)

1792 Elected Mayor of Norwich

JOHN HERRING & SONS

Shawl manufacturer

Gildengate

First noted 1806

1806 'Mr John Herring jnr. of Norwich exhibited 2 shawls [at the Holkham Shearing] manufactured by Messrs John Herring & Sons entirely from the fleece of Mr Coke's Southdown wool' (*Norfolk Annals*).

1807 'Mr Herring jnr. produced goods of his manufacture and stated that 117 shawls had that year been made from 224 lbs of Mr Coke's Southdown wool' (*Norfolk Annals*).

1851 Census: William Herring, aged 67, retired silk and worsted manufacturer.

HIGGINS & CO.

Shawl manufacturer

Pitt Street

First noted 1801

Last noted 1849

1849 'Various additions and improvements were made . . . by Higgins & Co. who brought the printed spun-silk shawl into notoriety' (*Journal of Design and Manufacturers*).

CHRISTOPHER HIGGINS

Manufacturer of shawls (1801); bombazine, crêpe and shawls (1822)

18 Coslany Street (1801) and Heigham (1822)

1813 Elected Freeman's Sheriff of Norwich.

1830 Shawlmaker, draper, chapman. Bankrupt. He 'traded by buying of silk and manufacturing the same into shawls and selling the same again as others of the same trade are used to do' (house deeds).

ROBERT HIGGINS

Shawl maker

First noted 1823

Last noted 1826

1826 Bankrupt and stock sold.

E & F HINDE
FRAS. HINDE & SONS

Manufacturer of light dress fabrics and shawls

Botolph Street

First noted 1810

Last noted 1927

1810 Firm started by Ephraim Hinde (1773–1857) with two sons, Ephraim and Francis.

1847 Registered three shawl designs at the PRO.

1847–8 Order book (H.10) in Bridewell Museum, Norwich, names thirty-three types of shawl, but most are unidentifiable today. Between February and July 1848, 13,134 shawls were made.

1862 Exhibited shawls and dress goods at the International Exhibition, London.

1862 Fras. Hinde & Son noted.

1878 Fras. Hinde & Sons noted.

1879 Moved from Botolph Street to St Marys Silk Mills (E & W L Burgess, *The Men who Made Norwich*).

1901 Became a Limited Liability Company.

Probable shawls: cat. nos 38–44 and 114.

Possible shawls: cat. nos 75, 76 and 123.

JOHN HUTCHIN

Bombazine, crêpe and shawl manufacturer

St James

Noted 1822

KEYMER & BAKER

Shawl manufacturer

22 Magdalen Street and St Saviours Back Street (Mrs Keymer)

First noted 1801

Last noted 1810

1803 Keymer signatory to the Wages Agreement as Master Weaver.

HENRY KING

Shawl manufacturer

Middle Street

Noted 1836

NICHOLAS KNIGHTS

Shawl manufacturer

Bishopgate Street

Noted 1801

P J KNIGHTS

Shawl manufacturer

2 Colegate and 11 King Street, Cheapside, London

1792 Won the Silver Medal of the Royal Society of Arts for his shawl counterpane (cat. no. 74).

1793 Her Majesty Queen Charlotte and the Princesses visit the Norwich Shawl Exhibition at 136 New Bond Street.

1794 Norwich Shawl and Fancy Waistcoat Warehouse, 4 Gentlemans Walk, opened 14 June 1794. Norwich Shawl Manufactory at: The Strand, London; 4 Gentlemans Walk; 2 Colegate. No. 2 Colegate was the manufactory of Alderman John Harvey; P J Knights, who started his career there, next moved to Gentlemans Walk and also had a showroom in The Strand. They all appear to have been known as the Norwich Shawl Manufactory.

1795 Opened shop in Milsom Street, Bath.

1809 Elected Sheriff of Norwich.

1833 Died in Greenwich.

WM LADELL & CO.

Shawl manufacturer

Calvert Street

First noted 1830

Last noted 1836

FRANCIS LADLEY

Shawl manufacturer

Lower Westwick Street

First noted 1799, St Swithins (Poll Book)

Last noted 1811

NICHOLAS MALLETT

Shawl manufacturer

5 Muspole Street

First noted 1801

Last noted 1819

Freeman 1802

Died 1819

1851 Census shows four generations all named Nicholas Mallett living at 67 Gilaken Yard, Heigham, and all weavers.

THOMAS MASSEY
Shawl manufacturer
10 Snailgate Street (later Pitt Street)
First noted 1801
Last noted 1836

MASSEY & ROBERTS
Shawl manufacturer
97 Pottergate
First noted 1801
1803 Signatories to the Weavers
   Agreement as Master Weavers.

WILLIAM METCALF
Shawl manufacturer
20 Colegate
First noted 1799
Last noted 1810
1800 Made a Freeman.
1803 Signatory to Wages Agreement as
   Master Weaver.

MIDDLETON, ANSWORTH & CO.
Manufacturers of light dress fabrics,
crinolines and shawls. Appear to have
concentrated on dress fabrics and
crinolines with shawls as a sideline
Calvert Street and Watling Street, London
First noted 1851
Last noted 1869
1862 At International Exhibition,
   London, showed 'rich Jacquard
   bordered shawl' and the 'brilliant but
   tasteful New Alhambra shawl'.
Possible shawl: cat. no. 68.

MATTHEW MIDDLETON
Shawl manufacturer
Colegate
Noted 1810

JOSEPH OXLEY & SONS
Cotton and shawl manufacturer
52 Gildengate (1801), Botolph Street
(1811) and Market Place (1817)
First noted 1801
Last noted 1818
1811 Cotton manufacturer at Botolph
   Street.
1817 Shawl warehouse, Norwich Market
   Place.
1818 New factory lit by gas.
Richard Oxley, son of Joseph, sold the
business to Willett & Nephew (no date).

THOMAS PAUL
Shawl manufacturer
1817 Bankrupt.

WILLIAM ROBERTS
Shawl manufacturer
Pottergate by Deep Bank
Noted 1810
1844 Died at Heigham, aged 87.

CHRISTMAS SAINT
Shawl manufacturer, dealer and chapman
1811 Bankrupt.

JOSEPH SEXTON
Shawl manufacturer
46 Snailgate Street
First noted 1801
Last noted 1810

SHAW & CRISP
Shawl manufacturer
Colegate
First noted 1845
Last noted 1848
1846 Registered one woven shawl design
   at the PRO.
1848 Registered one woven shawl design
   at the PRO.

RICHARD SHAW
Shawl manufacturer
St Georges; Colegate (1836, 1850) and
1 Milk Street, London (1850)
First noted 1822
Last noted 1850
1822 Manufactured bombazine, crêpe,
   shawls and camblets.
1830 Noted at St Clements.
1831 Owner of book of border designs
   bought for Strangers Hall in 1993.

SHICKLE, TOWLER & CAMPIN
Shawl manufacturer
Elm Hill and 48 St Pauls Churchyard,
London
First noted 1830
Last noted 1836

JOHN SINCLAIR
Shawl and bombazine manufacturer
Golden Dog Lane
1821 Leaves Norwich for London,
   'where he will carry on the bombazine
   and shawl trade, and will act as agent
   for any Norwich manufacturer'
   (*Norwich Mercury*, 29 September).

FREDERICK SMITH
1808 At Lord Somerville's annual spring
   exhibition 'Mr Frederick Smith
   exhibited specimens of ladies' dresses,
   shawls and stockings manufactured in

this city from the fleeces of His
Majesty's and Lord Somerville's
merino flocks' (*Norwich Mercury*,
29 September).
1809 Showed various long and square
   shawls all of Anglo-merino wool at
   Lord Somerville's exhibition, using
   English-grown Spanish wool, of which
   1 pound in weight measured between
   70 and 80 miles.

MESSRS SMITH, AMIS & CO.
Shawl and bombazine manufacturer
Noted 1820
1820 Sent Queen Caroline a piece of
   their flowered bombazine (*Norwich
   Mercury*, 5 August).

ROBERT SMITH
Shawl manufacturer
Tubby's Yard, Muspole Street
First noted 1836
1851 Census: a master shawl
   manufacturer living in St Helens
   Hospital.

JOHN SULTZER
Shawl and silk manufacturer
113 Botolph Street
1803 Born in Leicester.
1828 Moved to Lichfield.
1838 Mayor of Norwich, elected onto
   Town Council. Justice of the Peace and
   Chairman of Norwich Waterworks
   Company.
1846 Registered three shawl designs at
   the PRO.
1856 Founded the Norwich Crape
   Company.
1857 Employed 82 males and 186
   females.
1872 Death of John Sultzer. Norwich
   Crape Company did not cease trading
   until 1924.
Known shawl: cat. no. 133. Probable
shawl: cat. no. 132.

WILLIAM TAYLOR
Shawl manufacturer
1795 Notice to the Debtors and
   Creditors of William Taylor of the
   City of Norwich, Shawl Manufacturer.

JOHN THOMPSON
Shawl manufacturer
Snailgate (1810) and St Georges Colegate
First noted 1805
Last noted 1810

1805 Report of cotton twist stolen from Mr John Thompson.

1806 Advert for sale of house and complete workrooms in St Georges Colegate, suitable for the shawl business, a woolcomber or an extensive manufactory.

1809 Complaint against John Thompson heard at the Michaelmas Sessions for refusing to pay journeyman Thomas Harmer his full wages.

TOWLER, CAMPIN & CO.

Shawl manufacturer
Elm Hill and 46 Friday Street, London
First noted 1846
Last noted 1851
1851 At Great Exhibition showed 'fillover scarfs with silk ground; printed silk net shawl.'
Known shawls: cat. nos 13–23, 28–30, 32; and 33 (Towler, Campin & Monteith). Probable shawls: cat. nos 9, 24 and 27. Possible shawls: cat. nos 25 and 26.

TOWLER, CAMPIN, SHICKLE & MATTHEWS

Shawl and bombazine manufacturers
Elm Hill
First noted 1842
Last noted 1845
1843–5 Registered 149 woven and 190 printed shawl designs at the PRO.
1845 They 'manufacture 70 varieties of goods . . . employ 700, including 150 fillover weavers, 140 men and boys as winders, with other weavers at power looms' (Norfolk Chronicle, 25 January).
Known shawls: cat. nos 10, 12 and 31.

TOWLER, ROWLING & ALLEN

Shawl and dress manufacturers
Elm Hill and St James Factory
First noted 1852
Last noted 1869
1852 'For a long time this firm [the various Towler companies] was eminent for the production of embroidered mantles, various kinds of shawls, greatly improved in the manufacture, especially the gossamer printed shawls for summer wear.' (A D Bayne, An Account of the Industry and Trade of Norwich).
1862 International Exhibition Catalogue, Class 21, No. 4164: showed Grenadine, Tissue, Arab Sangiers shawls etc., both in plain and fancy styles composed of silk.
1869 Occupied second floor of St James Factory and hired two of the weaving sheds. Also noted at Elm Hill.
Known shawls: cat. nos 34, 35 and 36.

TOWLER & SHICKLE

First noted 1836
Last noted 1841
1840 Showing a 'fillover loom in operation manufacturing borders' at the Norwich Polytechnic Exhibition.

JAMES VINCENT

Shawl manufacturer
St Clements Church Alley
First noted 1807
Last noted 1822
1807 Notice of marriage of Mr John Towler, dyer, to Miss Vincent, daughter of Mr Vincent, shawl manufacturer of St Clements.
1822 Noted as bombazine, crêpe and shawl manufacturer.

WARREN & BATEMAN

Shawl makers
Calvert Street
First noted 1842
Last noted 1844
1844 Registered four woven shawl designs at the PRO.

WILLIAM WHITE

Shawl and scarf manufacturer
13 King Street
First noted 1877
Last noted 1883

WILLIAM WHITE & CHARLES WRIGHT

Hatters and hosiers
35 London Lane
First noted 1791
Last noted 1792
1791 'A Mr White endeavoured to produce an article striped with a coloured silk, silver and gold, but he did not succeed' (Mrs Barwell, A Companion to the Norwich Polytechnic Exhibition, 1840).
1792 Advertisement: 'Shawl Cravats, Sashes, Waistcoat Shapes, ⁶/₄ square shawls, ³/₄ and ⁴/₄ scarves and gown pieces in great variety' (Norwich Mercury, 1 November).

MARTIN WILLEMENT

Bombazine crêpe and shawl manufacturer
Bishopgate, Snailgate and Colegate
First noted 1794
Last noted 1824
1794 Advertises as owner of Norwich Shawl Manufactory (Norfolk Chronicle, 27 July). In the same year, sells his 'embroidered shawls'.

RICHARD GEORGE WILLEMENT

Shawl manufacturer
Church Alley St Clements
First noted 1830
Last noted 1863

MESSRS WILLETT & NEPHEW

Shawl and fabric manufacturer
Pottergate, 63 Friday Street, London and St James Factory
First noted 1824
Last noted 1889
1824 The unemployed weavers 'proceeded to Messrs Willett's factory in Pottergate where (these gentlemen being suspected of sending work out of the city) they demolished not only the windows but the floors of the lower rooms' (Norwich Mercury, 24 February 1826).
1828 'About the year 1828 power looms and Jacquard looms were, by the enterprise of Mr H Willett, introduced. The bigoted hand-loom weavers used great efforts to obstruct the use of these innovations and Mr Willett became so unpopular that at his funeral the mob tried to stop the funeral cortège' (W R Rudd, 'The Norfolk and Norwich Silk Industry', Norfolk Archaeology, 1923, no. 21).
1837 Henry Willett a member of the Committee for the formation of a School of Design in Norwich.
1839 'Henry Willett and his brother Edward carry on business on a very large scale having sometimes from 800–900 looms employed' (A Commission to Report).
1843 One woven shawl design registered at the PRO.
1869 Occupied third floor of St James Factory, with the Pottergate Factory as a base for the handloom weavers working from home.
Known shawls: cat. nos 99, 105 and 134. Probable shawl: cat. no. 104. Possible shawl: cat. no. 93.

Glossary

This chapter defines terms used in the book relating to manufacturing techniques, shawl designs and fabrics, and the principal types of Norwich shawl.

ADJECTIVE DYES The group of dyes which require the use of mordant salts to protect them from loss of colour through light and washing.

ARAB SHAWL Term used by manufacturers E & F Hinde for shawl resembling a burnous.

BALANCED WEAVE Any weave structure in which the warp and weft have equal weight and influence and give a 45-degree angle. Most noticeable in twill.

BATTEN The part of the loom which carries the reed and the shuttle race. It hangs from the upper frame or pivots from the base of the loom and is used for beating the weft into position.

BEAM Each loom has two horizontal wooden beams. The warp is wound on the front beam and the finished cloth on the back one.

BOMBAZINE Twilled fabric of worsted and silk (a half-silk) much used for mourning dress.

BORDERER Either a manufacturer or a weaver who makes narrow borders for shawls.

BRILLIANTS Glazed patterned worsteds similar to taboretts.

BROCADED SATIN Fabric with floral motifs formed by floating weft threads on a satin weave background.

BURNOUS An item of Arab dress incorporating a cloak with a hood. Fashionable as a European shawl or cloak worn by women, 1850–70.

BUTA (BOTEH) The Indian word for what is known in Paisley as the Paisley pine and in Norwich as the pine. The most common element in both Norwich and Indian shawls.

BUTTON LOOM A form of drawloom. The pattern shaft cords are lifted by the weaver and held in slots by 'buttons'. Limited in use to simple patterns.

CALLIMANCO Heavily glazed worsted of satin weave often striped in two or more colours.

CAMBLET (CAMLET) Worsted fabric of tabby weave, usually plain, but sometimes patterned, especially in stripes and checks.

CAMBLETEE Figured and glazed camblet.

CAMBRIC Cotton fabric in plain weave, coloured, striped, checked or plain. Also printed.

CANE Warp wound onto back beam of loom.

CANTON CRÊPE Plain woven silk fabric using good quality silk. Made in Norwich by Grout.

CARDING The process by which short-staple wool is passed over fine wires (cards). This produces a fine film of wool with the fibres lying at all angles. The resulting cloth will felt.

CASHMERE Wool obtained from the silky underbelly of the Tibetan goat.

CHALLIS A soft wool or mixed fabric used in dresses. Introduced about 1832 in Norwich. Thinner and finer than crêpe.

CHINESE ARCHITECTURAL Type of design used particularly on borders of turnover shawls in the 1820s and 1830s. The colours are clear and definite and the designs resemble chinoiserie.

CHINA CRÊPE The earlier name for crêpe de Chine. Not as expensive as Canton crêpe. Grout specialised in its manufacture.

COMBER BOARD A board perforated to separate and keep in order the heddles or leashes of the mounting on a drawloom or Jacquard loom. Also provides warp sett.

COMBING The combing of long wool fibres to lay them parallel before spinning into a smooth even thread.

CRAPE *See* Norwich crêpe.

CRÊPE DE LYON A short-lived fabric produced in Norwich in the late 1820s. Its structure is now unknown.

DAMASK Reversible patterned fabric, the pattern being made by the contrast between the warp and weft faces. Often self-coloured.

DENT The space between the teeth or leaves of the reed through which the warp ends pass in a loom.

DIAMANTINE Glazed worsted with diamond pattern.

DIAPER Linen or union fabric woven with a small geometric design which forms diagonal lines.

DOUPS Special heddles used in leno weaving.

DRAWBOY'S FORK A device invented to aid the pulling up of the drawcords. It consisted of a solid stand fixed near the loom, on which was mounted a heavy two-pronged block with which the drawboy could select and lever up the next row of pattern.

DRAWLOOM A handloom for weaving figured textiles, equipped with a special type of figure harness that controls some or all of the warp ends.

DRAWSTRINGS Drawstrings or tail cords are attached to the lingoes and by pulling them the warp ends are raised.

DRYSALTER A merchant from whom dyes, gums, oils and drugs were purchased.

DYES Dyestuffs which required mordants (fixatives) to protect the colours from fading or running. The main colours used in Norwich shawls, and the natural materials from which they were derived, are listed here:

Black From the galls of the oak tree (local); logwood from America.

Blue Indigo (imported); woad (grown locally). The dyes are extracted from the plants' leaves and stalks.

Brown Catachu from the Far East: a resinous substance obtained from the acacia catachu tree.

Purple Orchil, or archil, obtained from lichens grown in the Canary Islands and the Levant; cudbear, extracted from lichens grown in northern Europe, especially Scotland.

Red Madder from roots (grown locally); cochineal from insects; sumack from plant leaves; safflower from the head of the flower; annatto from the seeds of the plant – not widely used but mentioned in the 1867 dyers' book of E & F Hinde. Used with various mordants, these dyestuffs gave a wide range of reds. *See* Norwich Red.

Yellow From: weld (grown locally); old and new fustian from plants; quercitron, the bark of the American oak tree.

DYESTUFFS

Natural Colours obtained by processing roots, leaves, insects, lichens, barks.

Substantive Dyestuffs which colour fabrics without mordants.

Synthetic From 1856, when W H Perkin discovered how to make 'mauvine' from coal tar, the growth of chemistry speeded the development of man-made colours. Perkin developed the analine group of dyes, followed by alizarin and azo dyes.

END An individual warp thread.

EXOTIC FLOWER Designs with stylised flowers and foliage. *See* Naturalistic flower.

FIGURE Pattern created by drawloom or Jacquard.

FILLOVER The pattern woven or darned into the plain ground of a Norwich shawl, usually with wool.

FLOAT A thread of weft or warp which crosses a certain distance without intersecting the cloth.

FLOOR LOOM A loom which is operated by foot pedals or treadles.

FLORETTA Glazed worsted with patterns formed by different structures in a weft effect against a ground weave in a warp effect.

FLY SHUTTLE A method of hitting the shuttle quickly right across the loom, which increased the speed of handweaving. The shuttle, fitted with small runners, is specially designed to fit the shuttle race.

FOURTH *See* Quarter.

GAUZE *See* Leno.

GERANIUM RED A strong scarlet-red, in the later 1830s known as Norwich Red.

GLASGOW SHAWL The name by which an Arab shawl in Norwich is known in Paisley.

GRIFFE Part of the Jacquard loom, consisting of a rectangular frame with knife-edge bars which raises the selected hooks.

GROUND The warp and weft which make up the cloth into which the figuring is woven.

HALF-SILK Fabric in which silk is mixed with other yarns, either cotton, linen or wool.

HANDLOOM Loom worked by the hands and feet of the weaver and his assistants.

HARLEQUIN Shawls which have at either end patches of differing colours, either woven in or sewn on. These may be plain, or the background to arcading or other motifs.

HARNESSES The frames which carry the heddles. They are slung in the loom threaded with the warp ends and operated by the shedding mechanism in the order required by the pattern.

HARNESS CORDS *See* Leashes.

HATCHING Fine parallel lines on a printing block. Used to simulate twill weave on a plain fabric.

HEDDLE The cords or wires fixed to the harness or shaft through which the warp threads pass. Also known as leashes.

HOT-PRESSING Applying a glazed finish by compressing the fabric between iron plates heated in a furnace.

JACQUARD LOOM A loom developed from the drawloom in which the simple, lashes and drawboy are replaced by a mechanism employing punched cards for the automatic selection and pulling of the cords. Invented by Joseph Marie Jacquard in 1802, but not used in Norwich until about 1829.

JOURNEYMAN In any trade a man who has finished his apprenticeship but is not yet a master.

KEY PATTERN Usually named the Greek key pattern. A border pattern of interlocking right-angled motifs.

LEASHES Loops of cord suspended in the drawloom and Jacquard to hold individual warp ends, and passed through holes in the horizontal comber card. Also known as harness cords. Contain the mail (eye).

LENO A light open fabric, made by crossing one set of warp threads upon another. The crossed warps are held in place by the weft and crossed back before throwing the next weft. Also known as gauze.

LIZURES A word used in the early 19th century, meaning lease or warp threads.

MAUL The mallet used by the printer to stamp the image.

MEDALLION A medal or similar-shaped unit in a design. Also the Paisley name for a moon shawl.

MOON SHAWL An Indian design on square shawls where there is a central circle and a quarter-circle in each corner. Copied in Britain, Paisley naming it 'medallion' and Norwich 'pot lid'.

MORDANTS Minerals used as fixatives in dyes. The most commonly used were alum, chrome and iron.

MOUNTURE Harness in drawloom or Jacquard loom.

MUSLIN A fine loosely woven cotton fabric used for late 18th- and early 19th-century dresses.

NATURALISTIC FLOWER Flower designs which can be recognised as species. Used on shawls 1820–30.

NEW DRAPERIES Fabrics brought to Norwich by the Dutch and Walloon immigrant weavers in the late 16th century.

NORWICH CRÊPE

17th- and 18th-century Norwich crêpe Made from two different yarns, often silk and worsted twisted to unequal tension, causing the fabric to pucker. Made in colours and black, much in demand for mourning.

Norwich crêpe So-called and introduced by J Francis in 1819, a fine silk-and-worsted fabric dyed in many colours and finished to imitate satin. Short-lived fashion fabric.

'Modern Norwich crêpe' Introduced in the early 19th century. Made from pure silk gauze, mechanically crimped. Specifically for mourning.

NORWICH RED Trade name for geranium-scarlet dye. Scarlet dyeing was a separate branch of the trade, being easily injured by accidental contact with other solutions. The Norwich trade directories over the years list several specialist scarlet dyers. The *Norwich Mercury* of 29 February 1840 published a letter from C A J Piesse, Dublin: 'Messrs Sims Pitchford & Stark . . . their mode of dyeing Norwich Red and crimson still I believe, remains a secret with them'. The 1839 report mentions: 'Manufacturers in Edinburgh sent hanks of silk to Norwich to be dyed scarlet/red (*A Commission to Report on the Conditions of the Hand-loom Weavers*, 1839). The 1826 Crape Ball, with its request for scarlet-geranium to be worn, would appear to confirm the importance of the colour.

NORWICH STUFFS A generic term used in the 17th century for a specialist range of worsted fabrics sometimes incorporating silk yarn and often glazed. These were made in Norwich.

ORGANZINE A term applied to reeled or net silks in which several twisted strands are again combined (with maximum twist) into yarn suitable for warp.

PAISLEY Pattern consisting of variations in the Indian *buta*. Often it is difficult to tell the difference between a *buta* design on a Paisley shawl or that on one from Norwich or France.

PALMETTE A design element resembling a fan-palm leaf, used on shawls.

PATTERN SHAFTS Extra shafts originally used for brocade or patterning. In use, similar to the drawloom.

PAWL A lever. *See* Ratchet and pawl.

PENCILLING Dye colour put onto the cloth by brush after the main areas have been block printed.

PICK A single passage of the shuttle through the shed carrying one or more weft threads. Also, the weft threads so carried. Also known as a throw or shot.

PICKING STICK The handle centrally placed in front of the weaver which he uses to propel or jerk the fly shuttle in either direction.

PINE *See Buta.*

PLAIN WEAVE The most common weave structure in which each thread of weft passes over and under a thread of warp. Also known as tabby weave.

POPLIN FRANÇAIS A light-weight dress fabric. An example of giving an ordinary fabric a fancy name to help sales.

POT LID *See* Moon shawl.

PRINTING

Application Thickened dye stuff is printed on white cloth, fixed by steaming, then cleaned by washing.

Discharge Cloth is dyed then overprinted with dyes that contain a chemical which removes the dyed ground colour.

Resist The design is printed on the cloth using dyes or mordants which will 'resist' the colour when the cloth is dyed. Usually for designs on dark grounds.

Overprinting Colours are printed over dyed pastel-coloured cloth, which will affect the colours of the printed design.

PRINTING BLOCK Made from layers of wood pegged together with a carved wood surface which printed an image. The block could be inset with fine copper wire to print fine lines, or tiny pin heads to create half-tone effects. A felted block had a felt surface put onto the block to give better dye saturation when heavier colours were required.

PUGGAREES Light narrow scarves worn round a pith helmet by ladies in India. They tied at the back and the long ends floated in the wind. Many were made in Norwich.

PUNCH CARD Cards punched with holes and lashed into a continuous chain. The holes allow the spring-loaded needles of the Jacquard machine to remain forward and hook onto the rising griffe which then raises the required warp ends.

QUARTER (4TH) In the late 18th and early 19th centuries shawls were measured in quarters of a yard. A shawl 1½ yards wide would be listed as 6/4.

RATCHET AND PAWL The ratchet is a set of teeth in the edge of a bar or wheel, in which a pawl engages to ensure motion in one direction only.

REED Used to keep the warp ends evenly spaced and aligned. It is fastened in the batten and serves to beat in the weft.

REGISTER Marks on the cloth which act as a guide to the printer to show where he should place the following block as he builds up the design.

ROMAN STRIPE A striped design popular in the second half of the 19th century. The colours used are those of Italy, bright green, red and yellow generally on a black ground. Blue is sometimes added.

SCISSOR PATTERN A shape seen frequently in the shawls of 1850–70 woven by Clabburn, Sons & Crisp. It resembles a pair of curved scissors.

SETT The number of ends per inch, or centimetre, in the final cloth.

SHAFT *See* Harnesses.

SHAWLING Shawl fabric sold or used by the yard and made into dresses, waistcoats, furnishings, etc. Late 18th and early 19th century.

SHED The opening in the warp that permits the passage of the shuttle.

SHOOT Weft thread in the shuttle.

SHOT *See* Pick.

SHUTTLE A torpedo-shaped device for throwing the weft through and across the selectively opened warp.

SIMPLES Vertical strings hanging from the horizontal drawstrings. A Frenchman names Simblott connected the harness cords to a series of tail cords which were passed at 45 degrees via a pulley system in a box above the loom and were taken over horizontally to a convenient point (*c*.1603). Vertical cords called 'simples' were taken from these, secured to the floor, and the drawboy was able to work at the side of the loom instead of being perched above.

SIZE A gelatinous substance used for stiffening some fabrics while in the loom. Applied to the warp and later washed out.

SLEY Batten. There were many sley makers in Norwich as in other weaving centres.

SLIP Design embroidered by the Elizabethans, consisting of flower, leaf and root.

SPUN SILK Short fibres of silk produced as waste from various processes. After partial degumming these fibres are spun into a variety of yarns which are classed as spun silk.

STUFFS *See* Norwich Stuffs.

TABBY *See* Plain weave.

TABORETT Glazed worsted fabric with pattern formed by separate warp float on tabby ground.

TAPESTRY-TWILL The techniques used in India for weaving shawls, and in Europe for weaving tapestries, where each shuttle carries one colour and works only on that part of the design using that colour. Therefore there are no floats at the back of the work, but many shuttles may be in use at one time. Also known as tapestry weave.

TAPIZADO, TAPIZONNE Brilliantly coloured worsted with polychrome flowers.

THROW *See* Pick.

THROWN SILK After the twisting of silk filament yarns (known as throwing) the result may be poil, tram, crêpe, organzine, grenadine or cordonnet, all types of thrown silk.

THROWSTERER The workman who throws the silk.

TIERERS Girls or boys who brushed the dye onto the surface of the colour sieve to provide an even layer of colour on the block.

TURNOVER SHAWL A small square shawl with a plain centre and patterned border. Two adjacent sides of the border are sewn on one way and the other two in reverse. When the shawl is folded diagonally the four borders are arranged in a chevron down the wearer's back.

TWILL WEAVE Weave where a diagonal line is formed in the fabric. In each line of weft a different series of warp threads is covered, though always in the same relation. There can be 3/1, 4/2, 2/2 and other combinations.

TWILL-TAPESTRY *See* Tapestry-twill.

VOIDED That part of a design which shows up because it is blank. Frequently in Norwich shawls, pines are voided by leaving the shape plain with patterning either side.

WARP The longitudinal threads of a textile.

WEB The finished fabric on the loom.

WEFT The transverse threads of a textile which are carried in the shuttle.

WORSTED Yarn spun from long-staple, combed wool. The term is also used for the fabric made from the yarn.

YARDAGE In referring to shawls, one which is cut from a length of shawling, possibly with a border and fringe added, rather than one woven as a whole.

ZEBRA A shawl design, developed by Clabburn, Sons & Crisp in the late 1850s and 1860s, consisting of a series of definite or indefinite horizontal stripes.

Bibliography

PRINTED BOOKS AND JOURNALS

Allthorpe, Margorie, *A Happy Eye: A School of Art in Norwich, 1845–1982*, Norwich, Jarrold, 1982.

Ames, Frank, *The Kashmir Shawl and its Indo-French Influence*, Woodbridge, Antique Collectors' Club, 1986.

Aspin, Chris, *The Woollen Industry*, Princes Risborough, Shire Publications, 1982.

Barwell, Mrs, *A Companion to the Norwich Polytechnic Exhibition*, Norwich, 1840.

Bayne, A D, *An Account of the Industry and Trade of Norwich*, Norwich, 1852.

Bayne, A D, *A Comprehensive History of Norwich*, Norwich, 1869.

Beatniffe, R, *The Norfolk Tour*, 6th edn, Norwich, 1808.

Becker, John, *Pattern and Loom*, Copenhagen, Rhodos International Publishers, 1987.

Benson, Anna, *Textile Machines*, Princes Risborough, Shire Publications, 1983.

Benson, Anna and Warburton, Neil, *Looms and Weaving*, Princes Risborough, Shire Publications, 1986.

Blair, Matthew, *The Paisley Shawl and the Men who Produced it*, Paisley, 1904.

Blakely, E, *History of the Manufacturers of Norwich*, Norwich, 1851.

Broudy, Eric, *The Book of Looms*, London, Studio Vista, 1979.

Burgess, E and Burgess, W L, *The Men who Made Norwich*, 1904.

Bush, Sarah, *The Silk Industry*, Princes Risborough, Shire Publications, 1987.

Clabburn, Pamela, *Shawls: In Imitation of the Indian*, Princes Risborough, Shire Publications, 1981.

Clabburn, Pamela, *Norwich Shawls*, Norfolk Museums Service Information Sheet, 1987.

Coleman, D C, *Courtaulds*, vol. I, Oxford, Oxford University Press, 1969.

Cunnington, Phyllis and Lucas, Catherine, *Costumes for Births, Marriages and Deaths*, London, A & C Black, 1972.

Duncan, John, *Essays on the Art of Weaving*, Glasgow, 1807.

Dunsmore, Susi, *Weaving in Nepal*, London, British Museum Publications, 1983.

Edwards, J K, 'The Decline of the Norwich Textile Industry', *Yorkshire Bulletin of Economic and Social Research* 16 (1), May 1964.

Edwards, J K, 'Industrial Development, 1800–1900' in C Barringer (ed.), *Norwich in the Nineteenth Century*, Norwich, 1982, pp 136–59.

Encyclopaedia Britannica (3rd edn), 1797.

Encyclopaedia Edinensis, vol. II, 1827, p 458.

Fawcett, Trevor, 'Argonauts and Commercial Travellers: The Foreign Marketing of Norwich Stuffs in the later Eighteenth Century', *Textile History* 16 (2), 1985.

Fawcett, Trevor, 'Retailing Norwich Textiles in Bath 1750–1800', *Norfolk Archaeology* XLI (I), 1990.

Gale, Elizabeth, *From Fibres to Fabrics*, London, Mills & Boon, 1972.

Gilmour, David, *The Pen Folk: Paisley Weavers of Other Days*, Paisley, 1879.

Hecht, Ann, *The Art of the Loom*, London, British Museum Publications, 1989.

Hooper, L, *Handloom Weaving, Plain and Ornamented*, London, Pitman, 1926.

The Illustrated Exhibitor and Magazine of Art, vol. II, London, John Cassell, 1852.

Irwin, John, 'The Shawls of Kashmir', *Country Life Annual*, 1950.

Irwin, John, *The Kashmir Shawl*, London, Victoria & Albert Museum, 1973.

James, John, *The History of the Worsted Manufactures in England*, London, 1857 (reprinted, London, Frank Cass, 1968).

Journal of Design and Manufactures, vols I – V, London, Chapman & Hall, 1849–51.

Kerridge, Eric, *Textile Manufacture in Early Modern England*, Manchester, Manchester University Press, 1983.

Lévi-Strauss, Monique, *Vernis Cachemires, Projets Formachés Conservé au Musée du Vieux Nîmes*, Paris, Adam Biro, 1990.

Montgomery, Florence, *Textiles in America*, London and New York, W W Norton & Co., 1984.

Norwich Street Directories, W Chase, 1783; T Peck, 1802; C Berry, 1810; G Blyth, 1842; Mason, 1852; Roger, 1859. National Commercial Directory (Norwich Ed.), Pigot & Co., 1823; 1830; 1840.

Orford, Hugh, 'The Norwich Shawl', *East Anglian Magazine*, April 1969.

Ponting, K G, *Discovering Textile History and Design*, Princes Risborough, Shire Publications, 1981.

Priestley, Ursula, 'Norwich and the Mourning Trade', *Costume*, no. 27, 1993.

Priestley, Ursula, *The Fabric of Stuffs: The Norwich Textile Industry from 1565*, Norwich, Centre of East Anglian Studies, University of East Anglia, 1990.

Priestley, Ursula, 'The Letters of Philip Stannard, Norwich Textile Manufacturer, 1751–1763', *Norfolk Record Society*, LVII, 1992.

The Public General Statutes passed in the Fifth and Sixth Year of the Reign of Her Majesty Queen Victoria, 1842.

Reilly, Valerie, *Paisley Patterns, A Design Source Book*, London, Studio Editions, 1989.

Rock, C H, *Paisley Shawls*, Paisley Museum and Art Galleries, 1966.

Rossbach, Ed, *The Art of Paisley*, New York, Van Nostrand Reinhold, 1980.

Rudd, W R, 'The Norfolk and Norwich Silk Industry' *Norfolk Archaeology*, no. 21, 1923.

Scarfe, Norman and Wilson, Richard, 'Norwich's textile industry in 1784 observed by Maximilian Lazowski', *Textile History* 23 (1), 1992.

Shearer, David R, *Why Paisley?*, Paisley, Renfrew District Council Museums and Art Galleries Service, 1985.

Stacey, J H, *The Historical Account of the City and County of Norwich*, Norwich, 1832.

Stavenow-Hidemark, Elizabeth (ed.), *Eighteenth-Century Textiles: The Anders Berch Collection*, Stockholm, Nordiska Museets Förlag, 1990.

Taylor, Lou, *Mourning Dress*, London, Allen & Unwin, 1983.

Transactions of the Society of Arts, vol. VII, London, Society of Arts.

Victoria & Albert Museum, *Designs for Shawls: The Designs of G C Haité*, London, Webb & Bowyer/Michael Joseph, 1988.

Warner, Frank, *The Silk Industry of the United Kingdom*, London, 1921.

Yetimova, Louisa and Belogorskaya, Rina, *Russian Kerchiefs and Shawls*, St Petersburg, Aurora Art Publishers, 1985.

Young, Arthur, *A Farmer's Tour through the East of England*, London, 1771.

CATALOGUES

Catalogue of the International Exhibition, London, 1862.

The Crystal Palace Exhibition London (1851): An Unabridged Republication of the Art Journal Special Issue, New York, Dover Publications, 1970.

Lévi-Strauss, Monique, *Sale Catalogue: Cachemires Européens et Indiens*, Paris, Drouot-Richelieu, 1991.

Musée Historique des Tissus, *La Châle Cachemire en France au XIXe siècle*, Lyons, 1983.

Paisley, Past and Present: Exhibition Catalogue, London, Liberty, 1988.

Rudzki, Dorothy, *Ratti and Paisley*, New York, Fashion Institute of Technology, 1986.

Sellick, E H and Sellick, W A, *The Textiles of William Folliatt*, for an exhibition of his designs and textile collection at the Working Silk Museum, Braintree, Essex, 1993.

West Surrey College of Art and Design, *The Art of the Shawl*, Farnham, 1977.

MANUSCRIPT SOURCES

Bedford Record Office: 'The Journal of the Marchioness Grey', Ref. L30/21/3/8.

Bibliothèque Forney, Paris: 'The Mocassi Manuscript' (samples of Norwich Stuffs from the mid-18th century).

Bridewell Museum, Norwich: manufacturers' pattern books of the 18th and 19th centuries; 'Francis Hinde Papers'.

India Office Library, London: Moorcroft, W, 'Notice of particulars respecting the manufacture of shawls in Kashmeer', 25 April 1821.

Norfolk Record Office, Norwich: 'Business Papers of the firm of Stannard & Taylor, Norwich, Stuff Manufacturers 1751–1770'; 'The Patteson Papers'.

Norfolk Local History Library, Norwich: Berry, R G, 'Grout & Co: 180 Years of East Anglian Textiles'; Edwards, J K, 'Norwich in the Eighteenth Century', 1972; 'The Story of Norwich Silks, being a short account of the manufacture of silks by Fras. Hinde & Sons Ltd from 1810 to the present time'.

Paisley Museum, Renfrewshire: Cross, William, 'Changes in the style of Paisley Shawls. A lecture given in the Museum, Paisley, 1872'.

Victoria & Albert Museum, London: John Kelly's pattern books 1763 and 1767.

Newspapers

East Anglian Newspaper, (February 1832).

Norfolk Annals.

Norfolk Chronicle.

Norwich Gazette

Norwich Mercury.

Sydney Gazette (April 1803).

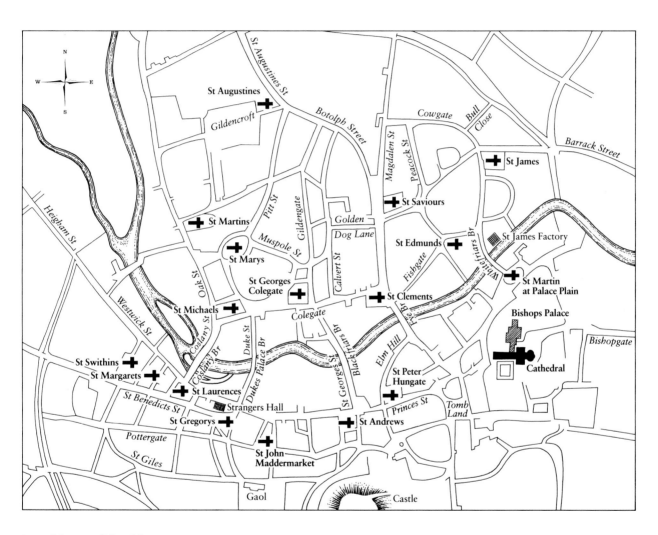

Map of the area of Norwich, to the north of the city centre, where most of the weaving, dyeing and printing of Norwich shawls took place. Based on John Ninham's map of 1802.